ASCD MEMBER BOOK

Many ASCD members received this book as a
member benefit upon its initial release.

Learn more at: **www.ascd.org/memberbooks**

BUILDING EQUITY

POLICIES AND PRACTICES TO EMPOWER ALL LEARNERS

DOMINIQUE SMITH · NANCY FREY
IAN PUMPIAN
DOUGLAS FISHER

ASCD | ALEXANDRIA, VIRGINIA USA

ASCD

1703 N. Beauregard St. • Alexandria, VA 22311-1714 USA
Phone: 800-933-2723 or 703-578-9600 • Fax: 703-575-5400
Website: www.ascd.org • E-mail: member@ascd.org
Author guidelines: www.ascd.org/write

Deborah S. Delisle, *Executive Director*; Robert D. Clouse, *Managing Director, Digital Content & Publications*; Stefani Roth, *Publisher*; Genny Ostertag, *Director, Content Acquisitions*; Julie Houtz, *Director, Book Editing & Production*; Katie Martin, *Editor*; Donald Ely, *Senior Graphic Designer*; Mike Kalyan, *Director, Production Services*; Valerie Younkin, *Production Designer*; Andrea Hoffman, *Senior Production Specialist*

PAPERBACK ISBN: 978-1-4166-2426-4   ASCD product #117031

PDF E-BOOK ISBN: 978-1-4166-2428-8; see Books in Print for other formats.

Quantity discounts are available: e-mail programteam@ascd.org or call 800-933-2723, ext. 5773, or 703-575-5773. For desk copies, go to www.ascd.org/deskcopy.

ASCD Member Book No. FY17-8A (July 2017 PSI+). ASCD Member Books mail to Premium (P), Select (S), and Institutional Plus (I+) members on this schedule: Jan, PSI+; Feb, P; Apr, PSI+; May, P; Jul, PSI+; Aug, P; Sep, PSI+; Nov, PSI+; Dec, P. For current details on membership, see www.ascd.org/membership.

Library of Congress Cataloging-in-Publication Data
Names: Smith, Dominque.
Title: Building equity : policies and practices to empower all learners /
   Dominque Smith, Nancy Frey, Ian Pumpian, Douglas Fisher.
Description: Alexandria, Virginia : ASCD, [2017] | Includes bibliographical
   references and index.
Identifiers: LCCN 2017016605 (print) | LCCN 2017029698 (ebook) | ISBN
   9781416624288 (PDF) | ISBN 9781416624264 (pbk.)
Subjects: LCSH: Educational equalization--United States. | Inclusive
   education--United States. | Education and state--United States.
Classification: LCC LC213.2 (ebook) | LCC LC213.2 .S64 2017 (print) | DDC
   379.2/60973--dc23
LC record available at https://lccn.loc.gov/2017016605

26 25 24 23 22 21 20 19 18 17   1 2 3 4 5 6 7 8 9 10 11 12

BUILDING EQUITY

POLICIES AND PRACTICES TO
**EMPOWER
ALL LEARNERS**

Introduction

A Chinese-American man dressed in workout clothes and flip-flops was on his way to the gym when he stopped by his local elementary school to enroll his son in kindergarten. The staff member at the front desk asked for ID and proof of residence. The man produced his ID and a utility bill, which his neighbors had assured him would be sufficient. The front desk worker apologized. The school needed to see a mortgage statement or rental agreement in addition to a utility bill, she explained. Two days later, this same man stopped by this same elementary school on his way home from work, dressed in a suit and tie. He had the required mortgage statement, but this time, the person working at the front desk asked only for a utility bill. His son was enrolled within minutes.

Some might look at this parent's experience and think, "No harm done." There was a minor obstacle, but eventually the man enrolled his son. Others see inequity—an example of the kind of bias that is all too common in schools. We don't know if the first staff member always requires two forms of documentation and the second only one, or if this parent's race and clothing influenced the treatment he received. What we do know is that he came away from the experience wondering why he was targeted and whether or not his son would be treated fairly in this new school.

A fair shot—that's what parents and students expect from their schools. Of course, some would not mind a little special treatment, but they believe that, at the core, schools have to be fair.

What it means for schools to be fair has changed over the decades. At one point in history, it was deemed fair to exclude girls from science classes. It was once considered fair to segregate students based on their race or ethnicity. Today, we think of fair as being not just equal but equitable. That's an important distinction. Whereas *equal* means everyone gets the same treatment and services as everyone else, *equitable* means each person gets what he or she needs to succeed. For example, in an equal situation, everyone running the race has shoes; in an equitable one, everyone has shoes that fit and are meant for running, as opposed to some having track shoes and others having shoes that are too small, boots, or high heels. In an equal school situation, we build staircases that learners can ascend to higher levels of achievement; in an equitable one, we make sure to build ramps alongside those staircases.

Equity in education is an important concern because schools are essential in the maintenance of democracy. Our founding fathers had two plans in place to ensure that the democracy continued. First was the three branches of government, and second was the need and commitment to educate citizens so that they would be sufficiently informed to participate in decision making. Our system of government is based on the idea that all people are created equal and have the same rights under the law. These are principles we teach our students, and they are principles we honor by working to ensure every student develops the skills and knowledge necessary to pursue his or her dreams.

School Equity

Imagine a school in which

- The student body truly *represents the diversity of human experience* and each member is being prepared to interact, survive, and thrive as 21st century learners and world citizens.
- The culture, educational program, and support services are *informed by and sensitive to the student body's social and emotional needs* such that each student is fully present and engaged in learning.
- The kind of opportunity roadblocks that cause the "haves" to receive more of what education has to offer and the "have-nots" to receive less have been identified and eliminated, and *all doors are open*

to opportunities to engage each student in challenging learning experiences.

- *Instructional excellence* is the norm, and each member of the instructional team is not just committed to professional mastery but also supported in a way that allows for its development and demonstration.
- The student body is *motivated and supported* to discover their passions and advance toward positive personal, familial, social, civil, and vocational goals and opportunities.

Now imagine transforming your school into one that is fully aligned with these principles and pursuing this overall vision. To that end, we have developed an organizational structure called the Building Equity Taxonomy (BET) and a set of aligned data-collecting tools—the Building Equity Review (BER) and Building Equity Audit (BEA). Our work to date in over 200 schools in Southern California and hundreds more throughout the United States encourages us to believe that this structure and these tools, applied in tandem, will help you clarify the equity concerns you have about your school and respond by initiating responsive equity-building practices. We offer this book to support your work to map a vision of equity for your school and promote concrete action to achieve it.

The Building Equity Taxonomy

The Building Equity Taxonomy (see Figure I.1) focuses on the equitable practices and outcomes that support critical standards of equity in a school or district.

As illustrated in the figure, the taxonomy has five levels, each of which will be explored further in the chapters to come:

1. **Physical Integration.** Equitable schools are diverse ones, and they value their students' differences and unique experiences with the world. In Chapter 1, we focus on integration efforts and broaden the lens from a focus on race and ethnicity to include class, gender, language, ability, religion, and sexual orientation.

2. **Social-Emotional Engagement.** Equitable schools address the needs of the whole child. In Chapter 2, we explore social aspects of the learning environment, including the creation of a welcoming climate as well as the value of restorative practices and efforts to improve student attendance.

3. **Opportunity to Learn.** Equitable schools analyze and challenge the structural aspects of the curriculum and identify areas that hinder students' opportunities to engage in deep learning. In Chapter 3, we focus on human and social capital within schools as well as compensatory and adaptive approaches to learning. We explore the ways in which school systems can provide students with opportunities based on *their* needs, which may differ from the needs of peers in the same class or school.

4. **Instructional Excellence.** Equitable schools provide all students with an excellent education that allows them to collaborate with other learners. In Chapter 4, we review the types of learning environments that students deserve—ones that include clearly articulated learning targets, well-defined measures of success, and tasks that are rigorous and aligned. We focus on the implementation of the gradual release of responsibility as a framework to ensure that students develop confidence and competence.

5. **Engaged and Inspired Learners.** Equitable schools see all students as capable and accomplished learners who are constantly building and reinforcing their identity and agency. Students are empowered to use their education to pursue new interests, skills, and aspirations, and the school provides support in the form of viable action plans and opportunities. In Chapter 5, we look at how students can learn to direct their own learning and identify what else they must learn to reach their dreams.

Each level in this taxonomy is an integral component of an equitable and excellent schooling experience. Unless all are addressed, schools will fall short of providing students with the education they deserve. For example, many

FIGURE I.1

The Building Equity Taxonomy

5. Engaged and Inspired Learners
Student voice and aspirations
Assessment-capable learners

4. Instructional Excellence
Gradual release of responsibility
Compensatory and adoptive practices
Professional Learning

3. Opportunity to Learn
Structural access to curriculum   Human and social capital

2. Social-Emotional Engagement
Cultural proficiency   Welcoming climate   Restorative practices   Attendance

1. Physical Integration
Race/Ethnicity, Ability, Gender, Class, Sexual Orientation: Broadening the lens

schools have achieved physical integration but have neglected to change the learning environment to a degree sufficient to promote the achievement of all students. Other schools have done admirable work to promote social and emotional learning but have not addressed curriculum and instruction or student engagement and inspiration. Still others have focused on providing quality instruction but not on ensuring this instruction is accessible to all students and that every child has the opportunity to learn.

This piecemeal approach to school equity has not resulted in outcomes that we can all be proud of. There are still far too many students whose aspirations are not realized, with dreams deferred or destroyed. We advocate for a much more comprehensive approach to equity work, one in which school systems consider every level of the Building Equity Taxonomy. It's a way to see equity not as "one more thing" but as *the* thing that drives a school's collective efforts.

A Means of Organizing Equity Concerns and Responsive Practices

Taxonomies have long been used in science to explain the world around us. A taxonomy identifies and separates things into groups and communicates the structural relationships that exist among these groups. Readers are undoubtedly familiar with Bloom's taxonomy and its 21st century update, which was proposed as a means of classifying educational learning objectives and then establishing and differentiating the relationship's among the groups of learning objectives based on relative complexity (Krathwohl, 2002). These groups of learning objectives were subsequently placed at different levels to indicate a hierarchical relationship.

Similar to Bloom's taxonomy, the Building Equity Taxonomy—with its five standards of equality and associated equity concerns and responsive practices—is organized into levels set in a hierarchical order. The order of the levels does not argue for the importance of one set of concerns and practices over another, nor does it imply that a school needs to completely address all issues located within the first level before attending to concerns and practices at the next. Rather, each BET level is presented in the order that we believe will promote practical progress toward equity. In other words, a school attempting to address concerns at the upper levels of BET will find limited success if it is ignoring many of the concerns at the taxonomy's lower levels. For example, BET Level 2 addresses the social and emotional needs of students, which is an equity concern based on the assumption that learners disengage when their social and emotional needs are unmet. BET Level 4 addresses access to excellent instruction, which is an equity concern under the assumption that educational achievement depends on quality instruction. Level 2 is a foundation for Level 4 in that students' ability to benefit from quality instruction will be magnified as they are socially and emotionally prepared to engage in their learning.

Even as we recognize the Building Equity Taxonomy as hierarchical, with each level providing an optimal foundation for the one above it, we caution against viewing the levels as a simple linear progression. For example, no school can afford to delay action to ensure quality instruction (Level 4) due to the fact that many students' emotional needs still require significant attention (Level 2). A trauma-informed school is still responsible for delivering quality instruction, and rather than seeing these initiatives as competing, effective schools work out the symbiotic relationships between responsive academic and nonacademic practices.

BET Level 5 (Engaged and Inspired Learners) does deserve a bit of special attention in this introduction. Levels 1 to 4 address equity concerns and practices that schools should consider when designing school equity plans. They focus largely on inputs—that is, on things the school might choose to do in order to promote a more equitable learning environment and experience. Level 5, in contrast, is much more focused on student outcomes—that is, on what educators hope to achieve as a result of their efforts to promote equity and excellence. Level 5 is about determining the effect of those inputs on the overall development and achievement of a student body. It's about asking, "How do we know whether our students have been affected by our responsive practices to further equity? Is our mission and vision for our school and student body truly being realized? What does a student demonstrate in skill, knowledge, and disposition that tells us our attention to school equity is approaching a quality educational experience?"

In order to conceptualize a response to these Level 5 questions, we looked to another taxonomy: Maslow's (1954) Hierarchy of Needs. In it, Maslow listed levels of needs that are foundational for the ability to realize and even transcend one's potential. He labeled his top level *self-actualization* and implied that meeting the four levels of more basic needs below it was the way to enhance one's ability to realize potential (i.e., to self-actualize) and then create new goals (i.e., to self-transcend). The analogy to education and to Building Equity Taxonomy was obvious to us, and we hope that as you read and discuss this book, it will become clear to you as well. Where Maslow's hierarchy is a psychological model that addresses conditions of a self-actualized person, our taxonomy is an educational model that addresses conditions necessary to foster an engaged and inspired student body. Maslow focused on four levels of basic human needs foundational to creating motivational drive and accomplishment; the Building Equity Taxonomy focuses on four levels of equity concerns foundational to fostering a self-actualized student body that is engaged and inspired to learn.

The Building Equity Review and Full Audit

As we have described, the taxonomy is a way of organizing equity concerns and responsive practices in a manner that promotes a school's ability to address them effectively. The Building Equity Review is a practical means to get that action under way. This 25-item, survey-driven tool gives school teams an entry point for their equity initiative (see Figure I.2). The statements, which are associated with specific levels of the Building Equity Taxonomy, target core, foundational equity concerns. Based on our experience, asking staff to explore agree/disagree responses to these statements is a good starting place for equity work. We hope that these 25 items, discussed in the chapters ahead, will help your school gather data on your strengths, generate a list of areas for potential growth, and engage in powerful and enlightening conversations.

A longer and more expansive tool—the full Building Equity Audit—is available for schools looking to move from inquiry to action. The audit consists of targeted surveys for staff and students. We've seen schools adapt these to provide a parent-focused survey as well, and we are working on developing a formal parent version of our own. You can find a copy of the staff and student versions of the Building Equity Audit in this book's Appendixes, along with links to download them. Like the shorter Building Equity Review, the

FIGURE I.2

Components of the Building Equity Review

LEVEL 1: PHYSICAL INTEGRATION

1. Our student body is diverse.
2. Our school publicly seeks and values a diverse student body.
3. Efforts are made to promote students' respecting, and interacting with, students from different backgrounds.
4. Our school facilities and resources are at least equal to those of other district schools.
5. Classroom placement and student schedules ensure that diversity exists in all learning environments.

LEVEL 2: SOCIAL-EMOTIONAL ENGAGEMENT

6. The social and emotional needs of students are adequately supported in the school, from prosocial skills development to responsiveness to trauma.
7. Teachers and staff show they care about students.
8. The school has programs and policies that are designed to improve attendance.
9. The school's discipline plans are restorative rather than punitive.
10. Students are treated equitably when they misbehave, and consequences are based on an ethic of care rather than demographic characteristics.

LEVEL 3: OPPORTUNITY TO LEARN

11. We do not use tracking to group or schedule students.
12. Students have equitable access to class placement and course offerings.
13. All students have access to challenging curriculum.
14. Teachers have high expectations for all students.
15. There are active working relationships between home and school to increase opportunities to learn.
16. Soft skills are developed and valued in our school.

LEVEL 4: INSTRUCTIONAL EXCELLENCE

17. All students experience quality core instruction
18. There are transparent and transportable instructional routines in place schoolwide.
19. Grading and progress reports are focused on subject matter mastery and competence.
20. Teachers notice students' individual instructional needs and have systems to differentiate as needed.
21. Educators have access to professional learning that builds their technical and intellectual skills.

LEVEL 5: ENGAGED AND INSPIRED LEARNERS

22. Students are engaged in a wide range of leadership activities within the school.
23. Student aspirations are fostered.
24. Students select learning opportunities related to their interests.
25. Students are provided authentic and applied learning experiences that link with their goals and aspirations.

survey items in the Building Equity Audit are organized by guiding statements that align with each of the Building Equity Taxonomy levels—from Level 1: Physical Integration through Level 5: Engaged and Inspired Learners. In addition, 25 key items from the full Building Equity Audit are discussed in Chapter 6 to provide further insight into the percentage of students who perceive themselves to be engaged and inspired learners.

When developing our equity audit tools, we borrowed from a progressive human resources employee evaluation practice called 360-degree feedback, in which one's performance is evaluated not just by a supervisor but also by peers, subordinates, and customers. Imagine a group of people standing in a circle and looking into the middle at the same event. Each of their perspectives on the event will be somewhat different, based on where they are positioned. The Building Equity Audit provides a way to solicit and combine the perspectives of various stakeholders (i.e., students, staff, and parents) into a full picture of equity concerns and responsive equity practices. In short, it can show you where the strengths and vulnerabilities lie so that you can move forward with better, smarter action.

The Building Equity Audit's greatest value is its ability to mine the perspectives and experiences that exist within your school right now in relation to each level of the Building Equity Taxonomy and identify which students are more prepared to benefit from current practice and which need additional support. To speak in metaphor, it can show you where a ramp should be provided alongside the stairs you've already put in place. The audit statements selected for inclusion in the Building Equity Review and discussed in this book are offered to provoke conversations, and the associated actions we propose focus on adding the right type of ramps so that more students can reach higher levels of attainment. A school's commitment to building those ramps, in essence, becomes its equity plan.

Conclusion

Progress toward a society in which all people recognize themselves as equals and respect one another's inalienable right to life, liberty, and the pursuit of happiness requires all of us to reexamine the distinction and relationship between equity and equality. It requires educators to challenge the institutional discrimination that still exists in our schools.

The pursuit of equity is not an easy path, and in many cases, it is realized as a "two steps forward, one step backward" process. But in order to move forward, even in fits and starts, we must understand where education as a field has been and what it might become.

Educational policymakers, researchers, leaders, and practitioners most often engage in this work by asking, "How are we going to ensure all students receive an equitable education?" In his brilliant 2004 book on community building, Peter Block points out that asking *how* is the wrong essential question. Before people can conceive of *the how*, he explains, they must first understand *the why*. That is, in order to figure out how to address inequity, we must understand why inequity exists—what we're doing or not doing that keeps it alive.

Why would anyone write a book about creating an equitable school without first addressing why equitable schools are important and what they might achieve? Why would *we*, who understand the importance of having a well-stated purpose for every lesson (Fisher & Frey, 2011), write this book without clarifying our intention? We know very well that the practice of communicating learning expectations and success criteria is highly correlated with instructional effectiveness and student learning (Hattie, 2009). Therefore, we chose to begin this book by clearly stating our purpose: *To extend the conversation about equity for all students and to provide educators with a comprehensive model for evaluating their current systems while providing a blueprint for improvement.* Our students deserve no less than a high-quality, inclusive, equitable learning experience.

Just imagine how different the world will be when children brought up to value individual differences grow up to run it.

CHAPTER 1

Physical Integration
Separate Is Not Equal

There's a verse in Bob Dylan's 1964 song "My Back Pages" that provided us with both confidence and a caution as we embarked on our school equity work:

> *A self-ordained professor's tongue*
> *Too serious to fool*
> *Spouted out that liberty*
> *Is just equality in school*
> *"Equality," I spoke the word*
> *As if a wedding vow*
> *Ah, but I was so much older then*
> *I'm younger than that now*

Dylan recognized that in the midst of the great civil rights awakenings of the 1960s, public education continued to be a hallmark of this country's commitment to life, liberty, and the pursuit of happiness. We can find a record of the hopes and expectations bound up in U.S. public education in letters exchanged by Thomas Jefferson and James Monroe. In these letters, each asserted the need and commitment to educate every citizen and expressed the belief that, as Jefferson (1787) wrote, education provides "the most security for the preservation of a due degree of liberty."

Like the protagonist of "My Back Pages," we have come to see the naiveté of assuming that the relationship between school equality and liberty is a simple or a linear one. Since Dylan wrote this song in the mid-1960s, there have been many policy-driven changes in public schools that have made them more equal, and yet widespread inequity persists. The words of the singer—wiser now, having shaking off the received truth of "self-ordained professors"—capture what we ourselves have come to believe through our work in schools: that a faithful focus on equality is not enough to promote liberty and justice for all. Equality is rooted in the concept of fairness, and a fair race is impossible when its various runners start at variable distances from the finish line, and the course takes them over very different terrains. Similarly, providing equal access to the stairway does not promote fairness to those who use wheelchairs. Achieving equity requires that this fact be acknowledged—and that we build a ramp alongside every stairway.

Without doubt, there are many groups that have been historically marginalized by both private sentiment and public policy. This deep-rooted marginalization is why both equality and equity remain critical concerns for public institutions, including our schools. Resources are not distributed equally among our schools, and some of the students who enter them are less prepared to benefit from the resources that are available. It's important to pause for a moment and considered how these concerns are intertwined. Advocating for advanced teacher education to support English learners (which is an equity-related resource that can help level the playing field) in a district's lowest-achieving school with its highest percentage of English learners may not address the underlying issue of low student achievement when the school is staffed with the district's least-experienced or least-qualified teachers (which reflects unequal distribution of resources).

Why Integration Is Important for Equity

The physical integration of students in classrooms and schools is foundational to the equity efforts that follow. Without a continuing focus on the inclusion of all children, it is likely that there will be an erosion of opportunity for some based on race, ethnicity, language, gender, and sexual orientation. Although physical access is not sufficient to ensure equity, it is an important consideration. There are still a lot of students who do not have the same access to their neighborhood school or public schools of choice that other students have. Physical integration is foundational to equity work because separate is not equal.

Taking Integration from Equality to Equity

Despite the framers of the Constitution's assertion that public schools were to be both the fuel and model of democracy, racial inequities have permeated and persisted in business, social, and governmental structures. There has been a pervasive movement to provide equal and equitable access to public education, fueled by a landmark Supreme Court ruling declaring that the doctrine of separate but equal had no place in public schools. This was followed by the Court's rulings requiring school districts to desegregate with deliberate speed. Thwarting these progressive efforts were 70 years of Jim Crow laws, pushbacks to forced and often poorly supported busing programs, and housing patterns that have maintained and increased the number of racially segregated neighborhoods. Whether it is a result of pervasive racism, poorly conceived public policy initiatives, or the effect of poverty and housing trends on school placements, the fact remains that the number of minority-majority schools is increasing, and that distinction continues to be a key indicator of educational performance. Despite notable exceptions, the more "separate" students are, the more unequal their outcomes remain. This is why physical integration is the foundational tier in the Building Equity Taxonomy.

Most of the policies and practices capable of rectifying aspects of inequity are beyond the purview of building-level decisions and, therefore, beyond the purview of this book. However, we must be aware that efforts to create more equitable learning environments will be limited by the extent to which schools remain segregated based on race, socioeconomics, and ability. These inequities must be addressed through progressive and institutional urban development, housing and educational policy initiatives, and structural changes designed to cope with the present-day effects of a long history of exclusion and segregation. We must remember, too, that the real goal to work toward is success for every student—and simply getting students in an integrated setting is insufficient to change the outcomes for many students. To truly level the playing field, educators must move beyond a focus on equality and start demanding equity. By focusing on equity, we expand our efforts beyond student placement. And in doing so, we can broaden our vision to include not only equity for students of all races and ethnicities but also for students of all socioeconomic statuses; degrees of language proficiency; gender identities; sexual orientations; and physical, emotional, behavioral, and intellectual abilities.

Broadening the Equity Lens: From Race to Identity

Over time, the recognition that separate schools could not be equal schools codified in *Brown vs. Board of Education* has evolved from a single-issue focus on race to conversations that include ethnicity, language, gender, sexual orientation, and disability. Whereas integration in U.S. public school was once primary about racially balancing a school's population of African American and white children, more recent explorations of identity have complicated the metrics of integration. First, we moved to consider an expanded number of racial and ethnic identities—Asian American, Latino, white, and Native American students as well as African Americans. Next, we opened our eyes to the numbers of low-income students, English language learners (ELLs), and students with disabilities. Now, we're factoring in intersectionality (e.g., Crenshaw, 1989; Jones & McEwen, 2000) and recognizing that our students are more than just a single racial, ethnic, or ability group assignment—that they have layered lives and affiliate with others through a complex mix that includes not only the aforementioned identities and the societal lens applied to each but also religion, geography, family relationship status, and age (see Figure 1.1).

FIGURE 1.1
Dimensions of Identity

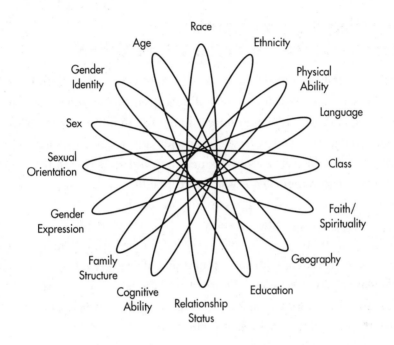

Source: Allegheny County, Pennsylvania, DHS LGBTQ Community Training Team/SOGIE Project Team. Reprinted with permission.

To provide just one illustration, a 9-year-old girl with Pacific Islander heritage living in Springdale, Arkansas (home to the largest expatriate population of Marshall Islanders in the world), is likely to experience schooling differently than a 9-year-old girl living in a community where hers is the only Pacific Islander family. The experience of this student would shift in all sorts of ways if her family were the wealthiest in the community or the poorest, if she were transgender, if she were gifted or had an intellectual or emotional disability, and on and on. Educators' efforts to improve the learning lives of all children must consider how dimensions of identity beyond traditional demographic measures can inform how we address social-emotional engagement, create more robust opportunities to learn, strengthen instructional excellence, and empower students.

Expanding the Interventions: From the Classroom to the Whole School

Ensuring equitable educational opportunities is a concern at both the school and district levels. Certainly there will be a need for targeted interventions, but creating a culture of achievement is an issue that touches the lives of all students, albeit in different ways. By broadening single-focus equity initiatives to comprehensive, schoolwide measures and approaches, we can make the practices that support equity standard practice.

Although the outward expression of inequitable practices may differ by group—for example, gender inequities look substantially different from limited opportunities to learn for black and Hispanic/Latino students living in poverty—each serves as a litmus test of a school's or district's responsiveness to the biases that its students experience. We can't move forward in discussing social-emotional engagement, opportunities to learn, instructional excellence, and student engagement and inspiration without first examining whom our efforts might affect.

Building Equity Review Statements: Physical Integration

It's time to delve into a discussion of the first group of statements in the Building Equity Review. These statements—and the examples we share of how teachers, administrators, and students we have worked with have responded to these statements—are meant to provoke conversation and kick off your equity work. Ultimately, we hope they will inspire your school to engage in the full Building Equity Audit and take targeted action.

As you review the set of statements associated with Level 1 of the Building Equity Taxonomy, keep in mind that physical integration is a necessary but singularly insufficient response to the equity crisis. Said another way, students have to be present in a valued learning environment, *and* we have to address their social-emotional engagement and their opportunities to learn. We have to ensure instructional excellence, *and* we have to give students voice while honoring their aspirations. To our thinking, this work starts with getting students in an integrated educational setting.

1. Our student body is diverse.

This statement asks teachers to consider what a diverse student body really is, with the reminder that that the definition of diversity should not be limited to a student body's racial, ethnic, or cultural composition. Ideally, a school should represent the diversity that exists in society. What complicates this ideal is that the immediate community and neighborhoods may not represent the diversity of society at large, and this is something the stakeholders in a school should bear in mind by considering who is represented and underrepresented. Knowing this is empowering, as it casts a light on who may be left vulnerable or isolated. Further, it affects the ways in which a school can address issues of fairness, privilege, and need. Awareness of diversity can generate ideas for supports, services, curriculum, and projects, and these ideas can find their way into equity plans that are generated throughout each tier of the Building Equity Taxonomy.

Sometimes physical integration is just a matter of an invitation. Members of the staff of Heritage Elementary School noticed that there were several neighborhood children who were being bused to another school that had a specialized class for students with significant disabilities. They talked with their principal about this, and she crafted a letter to these children's parents and guardians inviting them to consider enrolling their child at Heritage. As part of her letter, the principal wrote, "You may be asking yourself why our school decided to reach out to you. Simply said, our current students are missing the opportunity to learn from, and with, your child. There is a wide range of human experience that our current students are missing—and part of that is because your child is not in attendance here." Of the seven students whose families received the letter, four were enrolled immediately. The school asked for and received district-level support in terms of staff and professional learning, and the principal said that she was thrilled with the outcomes. The parents of the students with significant disabilities reported increases in their children's social skills, friendships, and academic performance, and there was widespread agreement among the Heritage stakeholders that this step toward increased integration enriched the learning experience for all.

2. *Our school publicly seeks and values a diverse student body.*

Regardless of the current demographics of your school, this statement prompts you to analyze the environment for evidence that educating a diverse group of students is important to the people who work there. There are any number of ways that a school can demonstrate its values, including inviting students who do not currently attend to join the campus, as the principal of Heritage did. Further, when staff members step up to point out that their school does not represent the diversity found in the community and advocate for change, it sends a clear message that all students are welcome.

The staff at Valley View Elementary School post signs around the school in Korean, even though they have only a few enrolled students who speak the language. As one of the teachers noted, "Language and culture are interconnected. When people see their language, they feel more comfortable. It's like we're saying, "We value you here." The teachers know that there are many more Korean-speaking students in an adjacent community, and they want everyone to know that they are welcome. The parents notice. One was overheard saying, "They take the time here to make you feel important. All of the directions and signs are in Korean, not just English and Spanish. I've told my friends that they should think about coming to this school." Valley View staff are quick to point out that this isn't about enrollment competition but about clarifying to the community that every child matters.

The signs in Korean are just one way that the staff at Valley View have publicly expressed their support for educating a diverse group of students. They also recognize that a significant percentage of their students live in poverty, and they have taken steps to show these students and their families that they are important in the school community. As one outward expression of this, Valley View installed washing machines and dryers in a former staff room so that parents could clean their children's clothes at no cost (a small community grant covers the expense). While the clothes are being washed, parents are invited to attend language development classes or financial literacy seminars or to volunteer in the classrooms.

Sometimes, staff education is a necessary precursor to publicly valuing a diverse student body. When Kennedy Middle School first began seeing female Muslim students wearing the hijab, or traditional headscarf, several staff members went to the administration with concerns. As one of the teachers wondered, "If Rabab can wear the hijab, what other things will students want to wear? I can just see my boundary-pushing kids saying they want to wear ski masks or pajamas all day. Does this mean our dress code will go right out the door? It clearly says that there are no caps, hats, or bandanas allowed."

Understanding that there was both a lack of information and a bit of fear behind such remarks, two history teachers invited a local Islamic religious leader to the school—setting up a completely voluntary after-school informational session for all staff. Attendees were urged to ask questions and to learn more about the traditions valued by Muslims. The teacher who made the comment about her student Rabab said afterward, "I had no idea that wearing the hijab was a custom, like wearing the cross is for me. It's not some random thing; it's part of a religious tradition. I feel bad for suggesting that it was just in defiance of our dress code."

The Valley View staff decided that they needed to update the dress code, which they did. But even more important, they decided to update their promotional materials to feature photographs of Muslim students wearing the hijab. They also scheduled a series of public seminars for the community and assemblies for students to facilitate their understanding of Islamic traditions. This last action generated some pushback from other religious communities, and the staff decided to host an annual Day of Understanding that would allow people to learn about cultures and traditions present in the community that are different from their own. The staff also invited religious leaders to attend the student-focused events and changed the emphasis from Islamic traditions to comparative religion.

3. *Efforts are made to promote students' respecting, and interacting with, students from different backgrounds.*

The whole idea of integration is for diverse groups of students to interact with one another. Unfortunately, in a lot of integrated schools, students form groups in which membership is defined by ethnicity, language, gender, or some other demographic.

The staff at Red Canyon Middle School noticed that parts of their school were highly segregated, despite the fact that their school represented the larger community well and was demographically very diverse. A look into the lunchroom highlighted this fact. In one area, all of the students were black. In another area, all of the students were Latino. Students did not interact across racial/ethnic lines during lunch or, the staff also noted, on sports teams or at social events such as dances.

When this student self-segregation was brought up during a faculty meeting, one of the teachers commented, "The kids are integrated during their classes. I think that they can choose to be with their own kind during their free time if they want." There was an audible gasp in the room, then a long pause. The teacher who had made the comment continued, "What? Don't students have the right to choose their friends?" After another long pause, another teacher responded, "Yes, students should be able to choose their friends. But I wonder what we're doing or not doing that means they don't have friends across races and ethnicities. There wasn't a single black kid sitting with a white or Hispanic student at the last dance. Why is that? It's bigger than student choice. It's an unwritten rule at this school that we need to change."

And change it they did. It started with a series of race and human relations lessons, which was followed by a mandatory interdisciplinary unit on individual differences. The staff at Red Canyon made a conscious choice to help students interact with a broader range of peers. They engaged students in discussion about their observations and held forums to gain further student feedback. The teachers emphasized more collaborative learning opportunities and problem-based group projects in their classrooms. It took time, but the results were impressive. Not only did the school's achievement scores increase, but so did student satisfaction. On Red Canyon's annual student perception survey, participants noted feeling safer at school and feeling more connected with fellow students and staff. Looking back on the progress the school had made, one of the faculty noted, "It was just something we missed. We had an integrated school but not an integrated experience. When that changed, this school became a better place for students to learn."

In addition to facilitating interactions, equity-conscious schools ensure that students feel respected for who they are. This requires careful attention to bullying prevention and addressing harassment when it occurs. We will focus on repairing harm in a later chapter in this book, but right now, we want to say a little about helping students learn to respect one another. Lack of respect can be displayed in many ways, and it can affect a wide range of students. For this example, we'll draw on the experiences of Danielle, who started a new school year by asking teachers and students to call him Danny and change the pronouns they used to refer to him from "she" to "he." Danny's choice was hard for some students and staff members to accept, as it violated their sense of right and wrong. In fact, after a great deal of soul-searching, one of the staff members at Danny's school actually transferred to another school, saying, "I can't accept Danielle as a boy, but I don't want to be part of the problem for her, or him, or whatever."

Other staff members recognized Danny's transition as an opportunity to teach respect. The English team purchased a number of adolescent literature titles that included transgender characters, such as *Luna* (Peters, 2004), *I am J* (Beam, 2012), and *Some Assembly Required: The Not-So-Secret Life of a Transgender Teen* (Andrews, 2014). They informed the students that the books were available for those who were interested. After a parent complained about *Luna*, staff scheduled a meeting with that parent and opened up a discussion of literature's role in helping readers understand the world around them. As one of the English teachers said, "The fact is that Danny goes to school here, and some students want to understand his life a little better. We didn't assign this book or any of the other new books that include transgender characters, but we did make them available so that students could become informed." Over time, Danny taught his peers and teachers that he was more like them than he was different. He wanted a good education and a fair shot at life. He wanted to be understood and respected. School became more equitable for him when his teachers accepted him and helped other students respect him.

4. *Our school facilities and resources are at least equal to those of other district schools.*

One of the ways that school systems telegraph messages about who is valued and who is less valued is through the facility. Within the same district, there can be significant disparities between the facilities available for students. Of course, when new schools are built, they are frequently better than older facilities; that's typically just the reality of new construction. The question is not whether the district's newest campus is "the same" as its oldest campus, but rather what is being done to modernize every campus and whether the expenditures for these facilities are available for public scrutiny.

The coaching staff at Johnson High School could not schedule night games because the school's athletic fields did not have lights. When asked about this, a district official tried to explain away the inequity. "When this campus was built," he stated, "the perception was that it was not safe [to be in this community] at night, so they didn't install lights." A school built around the same time, only seven miles away, had lights for its athletic fields, so the students from Johnson were bused to that school for evening practices and games. Just think about the message this sends students and their families.

It took the alumni association to kick off change. Former students raised several thousand dollars, and the district matched the funds so that Johnson could have lights installed on its sports fields. The pride the students felt on the first night of a genuine home game cannot be overstated. As one of them said, "I'll remember this for my whole life. People cared enough for me to have a win in my own neighborhood."

Of course, facilities are more than sports fields. When the teachers at Avondale Elementary completed their Building Equity Audit, they noted that most other schools had replaced computer labs with laptop carts that travelled from classroom to classroom. "We lose a lot of instructional time walking from class to the lab," one teacher noted. "The computers in the lab are outdated, and our kids only get to use them every so often, when we sign up. It doesn't seem fair that other schools have updated their technology so much more than we have."

When Avondale staff contacted the district office, they learned that there was a technology phase-in plan in place and that they would eventually get new tools for their students to use. The principal, advocating for students and teachers in terms of equity, asked if there was a way to accelerate the process. In response, the district technology staff said yes, but that would mean that the work would have to be done while students were in session rather than during the summer break. The staff readily agreed, and the school had updated technology months ahead of schedule. It was wrong for Avondale students to have waited as long as they did, but coordinated action between motivated educators and the district meant they would wait no longer.

5. Classroom placement and student schedules ensure that diversity exists in all learning environments.

Getting students into neighborhood schools that value diversity is a worthy goal and has been the focus of much of the school equality work of the past several decades. However, once students are on the campus, they are often at risk of being segregated. As we noted in an earlier section, sometimes students do this themselves as they form their friendship groups. In that case, educators can intervene to provide students with opportunities to get to know a wider range of people. Other times, it's the educators who segregate students. We have to believe that they do so with good intentions, despite the fact that separate remains unequal. Sadly, this is all too common, so we'll spend a bit more time providing examples of what teachers and administrators have done to address within-school segregation.

Perkins Elementary School has a group of students who live in poverty. The number isn't big enough for Perkins to have a schoolwide program, so the staff decided to schedule a reading intervention class for students who qualify for Title I services. Every day at 9:35 a.m. or 11:00 a.m. (depending on the grade level), targeted students left their regular class to be taught in small groups by a reading specialist. The staff tried hard to ensure that only students who qualified for the added intervention received it, but in doing so, they segregated students based on family income. Meanwhile, missing regular lessons led many of these students to fall further behind in class, despite the intervention intended to support their achievement.

When the Title I teacher retired and a replacement was hired, he asked if his schedule could include time to provide support for students within their regular classes. In a discussion with a group of 1st grade teachers, the new Title I teacher said, "I think we could have more success if students had access to your content with my support rather than two different contents to try to learn." This advocacy for equity dismantled the inadvertent segregation that had occurred at Perkins. For example, while the class was engaged in collaborative learning, the Title I teacher invited four qualified students to meet with him for an additional reading lesson, which was based on the lesson that the classroom teacher had previously taught. In the first year of implementation, the scores for students who qualified for Title I services increased by 18 percent, and the teachers attributed this to the increased amount of instructional time that students experienced, as they no longer had to travel to another room or miss out on core content. In addition, they noted that "the Title I interventions were directly connected to what students were supposed to be learning and students could catch up faster when the Title I teacher based his lessons on areas of student need from those lessons."

Another form of within-school segregation that merits careful examination is the practice of single-sex, or gender-separated, education. We saw this at Westfield Middle School, where, to combat chronically low science achievement, the teachers decided to create optional "girls only" science classes that girls could enroll in with parental permission. For us, this is kind of gender-based segregation is problematic. We recognize that this is a controversial stance and that there are individual studies that demonstrate some positive effect on learning for some students in classes set up this way. Still, Hattie (2009, 2012) reports no supporting research-based evidence for the benefits of gender-segregated education. In other words, there is a lack of compelling evidence to suggest that gender-based classes significantly improve long-term learning.

Students with disabilities are another group that is often segregated within a school. We have lost count of the number of times we have been told that segregating students with disabilities in self-contained classrooms was "for their own good." Again, if there were data demonstrating that segregating special education students and teaching them separately led to significant improvements in learning, we'd stop talking about this. But that is not the case. Even a cursory review of outcome data from special education classrooms clearly indicates that students with disabilities have a long way to go to learn at reasonable levels. The least dangerous assumption we can make is that students with disabilities can and should learn alongside their peers without disabilities, and that specialized supports can be provided within the context of the regular school day.

There is still a significant bias in the teaching profession about responsibility for students with disabilities, whether the disabilities are intellectual, behavioral, emotional, or physical. Some special educators have the mindset that they, and only they, are qualified to teach students with disabilities. Some general educators believe that they don't have the skills to meet the complex needs of students with disabilities, and that the result will be a bad educational experience for all students in the class. The reality is that there is no secret knowledge that special educators are keeping hidden from general educators. Good teaching is good teaching; it's just that some students might need extra support and time to learn.

Laurel Academy High School had maintained segregated special education classes for many years. Students with disabilities were routinely educated with peers who also had disabilities. As one teacher noted, "That's just how it always was. We never even thought to ask about this until we started working on our Building Equity Audit. Suddenly we realized that there was a group of students who had been left out of our discussions. It was a wake-up call for us to realize that all of our previous efforts had neglected an entire group of students."

As we have noted before, recognizing the problem is important, but it's figuring out what to do in response that's critical. Given that each of Laurel Academy's students with disabilities had an individualized educational plan (IEP) that indicated his or her placement, the staff could not make unilateral or rapid changes in this area. Instead, they focused on talking with parents and teachers about designing systems of support so that these students would be successful.

When we talk about the changes at Laurel Academy, people tend to wonder about the "appropriateness" of the students with disabilities being educated in regular classrooms. As one person said, "After all, at the IEP team meeting, all the stakeholders decided that the separate learning environment was the best placement." There is a surface logic to that argument, until you realize that placement decisions are typically based on recommendations of what is known rather than what can be realized. If type or severity of disability were a good predictor of who could, or could not, be educated in a regular classroom, there would not be significant disparity in rates of integration and inclusive education. But there is. District to district and state to state, the percentage of students who are educated 80 percent or more of the school day in the general education classroom varies widely, which suggests that the sophistication of the system, rather than the student himself or herself, is the variable that facilitates (or blocks) access to a quality education in the regular classroom.

As with getting students into a diverse school, simply getting students with disabilities into regular classrooms is a necessary but singularly insufficient step to achieving equity. From there, the work becomes more focused on ensuring the proper systems of support, which we'll look at in this book's remaining chapters. A student with a disability who is educated by a special educator is not receiving the same education as a student who has access to a general educator. The knowledge base is different. Similarly, a student with a disability who has accommodations and modifications designed by a special educator is more likely to achieve equitable outcomes than a student who does not receive accommodations and modifications or whose accommodations and modifications are designed by someone without formal training.

First Steps: It Starts with You

Knowledge is power. Isn't that what we tell our students? But what is your level of knowledge about the place where you work and teach? You can become better acquainted with district decision making by attending at least one school board meeting this year to learn about the critical choices facing your community. You can ask a student and his or her family to lead you on a walk through their neighborhood. The view from the sidewalk is much richer than the one we see through the windshield. Try attending a community festival, meeting, or religious celebration that you wouldn't otherwise attend. Take your own personal action to become better informed about life outside of your classroom or school.

Conclusion

Court decisions and legislative actions resulted in efforts to physically move historically marginalized students into school communities that offered greater opportunities. These efforts continue today in programs such as magnet schools that integrate schools racially and ethnically, and in inclusive school practices where students with disabilities are educated alongside students without. The rationale behind these practices is a concern for the benefit of the individual student combined with an appreciation of the transformative effect that his or her inclusion can have on the culture of whole school and the individual classroom. The statement "Separate is not equal" does not imply that physical integration alone will increase student achievement and empowerment. Instead, your equity audit may identify practices that need to be changed so that children will learn effectively together. Engaging in such practices will give students access not only to the stairway but also to other ramps they need to reach their goals. This perspective is further embodied in the guidelines of how a school should run and what supports should be in place to make the environment one of learning and safety for all.

When we focus on school reform, we cannot limit our attention to the day-to-day procedures and policies of the school; we must broaden our vision to include understanding how outside factors play a part within school life. We need to start to focus on how students are affected by outside influences and how those influences affect the inside culture of the school.

CHAPTER 2

Social-Emotional Engagement

Students Don't Care How Much You Know Until They Know How Much You Care

Pin Oak Elementary School is known throughout its suburban community for putting out the welcome mat. All the traditional efforts are in place, like the bulletin board in the main office that says "Welcome!" in the 12 languages represented within the student body, but Pin Oak staff and parent groups go above and beyond to ensure that the daily practices of the school match their stated values.

"It's easy to be welcoming when all is well," said Lorena Fonseca, president of the school's parent-teacher organization (PTO), "but we have to be welcoming when things aren't so good, too. That's what being a family is really about." Ms. Fonseca rattled off a list of practices at Pin Oak: the committee of educators and parents focused on restorative practices (Smith et al., 2015), a bilingual social worker who meets with the families of students experiencing attendance problems, and a female vice-principal who meets off campus with a group of Muslim mothers because that's how they prefer to interact with the school. "We've also done away with 'Donuts with Dad' and 'Muffins with Mom,' because we realized we were excluding families that couldn't participate in that way," she explained. "Now we have 'Breakfast Bunch' and invite children to invite anyone who loves them."

What Pin Oak is doing isn't extraordinary. Practices like these quietly take place every day across the United States. Pin Oak is located outside a large city, and in recent years its suburban district has seen the student population grow more diverse. The staff is committed to being responsive to the needs of the community. Along with countless educators everywhere, they are examining how to best serve and support their students and those students' families, and this sometimes means altering long-held policies. For example, not so long ago, Pin Oak used conventional discipline approaches that did not involve the family. "They'd just call and tell you what had happened and what the punishment was," said Ms. Fonseca, whose children have attended Pin Oak over a span of 10 years. Chronic attendance problems were handled by a district school attendance review board, with little direct school involvement to address long-term problems like physical or mental health issues in the family.

"I think the biggest change for me was coming to understand how other families participate in their child's schooling. I used to believe that if you weren't here, if you didn't show up to PTO meetings and events, it meant you didn't care," Ms. Fonseca said. When families from East Africa began moving into the community, the principal and parent-leaders met with the local imam to better understand their concerns. "That's actually what inspired the off-campus gatherings," she said. "It's given these moms a chance to extend their hospitality in the school's direction. I go to these meetings, too, so I can come back here and serve as a voice for them."

The social-emotional engagement of students, long understood to be critical to academic progress, is an essential element in developing equitable schools. In their review of the social-emotional elements that factor in achievement, Becker and Luthar (2002) highlighted these four as the most influential: (1) academic and school attachment, (2) teacher support, (3) peer values, and (4) mental health. Many well-meaning academic interventions have focused on content and instruction, but these programs have limited impact when the social-emotional lives of children are not taken into account.

Of course, fostering social-emotional engagement requires more than a few freestanding lessons on character and decision making with little follow-up after the lesson. In order to improve social-emotional engagement, schools and districts must do what Pin Oak Elementary has done: examine policies and procedures, build practices that foster relationships, and align discipline such that students are able to use the communication and interpersonal tools they are being taught (Collaborative for Academic, Social, and Emotional Learning, 2015). In this chapter, we will describe these dimensions more fully in our discussion of cultural proficiency, a welcoming climate, restorative practices, attendance, and response to trauma. We'll begin as Pin Oak Elementary did, with attention to cultural proficiency.

Why Social-Emotional Engagement Is Important for Equity

Schooling is a human endeavor, and one that is sustained by the reciprocal trust among educators, students, and families. These relationships are complex and ever-changing, and can be bolstered or harmed by the words and actions of the various parties. Therefore, it is essential for the school to intentionally create systems that support the social-emotional engagement of its members and help them to feel understood and valued. When organizations naively overlook the importance of the culture and experiences of its members, relationships suffer. When there are no mechanisms to repair relationships, hearts harden and so do inequities. The school becomes a hierarchy of insiders and outsiders, with those who are marginalized turning away from the potential that partnerships could offer.

Culturally Proficient Schools

As communities evolve and demographics change, schools and districts are charged with reshaping their practices to best meet the needs of the students and families they serve. It's worth noting that this statement marks a paradigm shift from decades past, when it was expected that the community would adjust to the norms of the unchanging institution.

Of course, adherence to "the old ways" can persist when staff lack the cultural competency necessary to understand the students attending their school and rely on their own personal experiences as the lens for sense making. This is more likely to happen in schools where there is a mismatch between the demographics of the students and the staff, and that kind of mismatch has become fairly common. Consider the numbers in California, a highly diverse state. In the 2015–16 school year, 41 percent of school and district staff (administrators, teachers, office clerical workers, and paraprofessionals) identified as white/non-Hispanic. However, only 24 percent of the state's students identified similarly. The largest student group, Hispanic/ Latino, comprised 54 percent of the public school enrollments but only 18.6 percent of the staff (California Department of Education, 2016).

Keep in mind that these numbers represent all adults who work in California's public school system, not just classroom teachers. The presence of every adult matters, and every adult can have a position of influence. This is why schools must invest in developing the cultural proficiency of every adult in the school, not just the teaching staff. After a series of workshops and discussions on cultural proficiency at our school, the cafeteria manager and the front desk coordinator, unbeknownst to any of us, examined their own practices to strengthen the responsiveness they could bring to our school and students. In short order, they had arranged for a vegetarian entrée option to be served each day at lunch—a change from the old way of providing a vegetarian option only on "Meatless Mondays." Broadening students' choices in the cafeteria may seem to be a relatively minor change, but consider how important food is when you are a guest in someone's home. Anyone who has had his or her dietary needs ignored by the host knows how marginalizing it feels to discover you can't eat what is being served.

In no way do we want to suggest that belonging to a particular race or ethnicity means you are culturally competent. Each of us exists in what Ross (2013) refers to as "cultural bubbles" that are informed by the unique intersectionality of our identities:

> For educators, unbroken "bubbles" are particularly troublesome. Our worldview becomes a paradigm that too often typecasts different as deficient... We carry with us value systems, expectations, and unrecognized stereotypes

of our worldview into our work with children and families, seeing their deficits rather than their strengths. (p. 2)

Much has been written about creating culturally proficient schools and pedagogy (e.g., Ladson-Billings, 1995; Lindsey, Robins, & Terrell, 2009), but like all equity work, this work begins with the willingness to self-reflect—to identify and acknowledge our own cultural bubbles. The importance of continuously posing questions to ourselves as institutions and as individuals grounds the work of becoming more culturally proficient. Lindsey, Kearney, Estrada, Terrell, and Lindsey (2015) suggest several questions that schools and districts can use to explore this topic:

- *"Who are we?"* or *"Who am I?"* This calls on groups or individuals to explore their sense of self. Knowing who we are and how we define what it means to be us helps us to understand that others have different values and perspectives. Coming to appreciate these differences facilitates cultural proficiency and competence.
- *"Why do we do what we do?"* or *"Why do I do what I do?"* These prompts call for the exploration of values, beliefs, assumptions, and meanings. Understanding that our values are steeped in culture allows us to consider that others have equally valuable values, beliefs, assumptions, and understandings of the world.
- *"How will we develop and use skills that we have?"* This calls on individuals and groups to explore their current capabilities and think about how to apply them to acquire new knowledge, understanding, and skills. In considering personal skills, individuals identify the skills and capabilities they do have, and how these skills can be developed to foster connections with others.

Having reflected on and shared the outcome of questions like those listed above, staff can explore two other key questions advocated by Lindsey and colleagues (2015):

- *"In what specific behaviors will I or we engage?"* This prompt is about exploring actions and reactions. It moves us beyond our bubbles as we work to change our behaviors to be more culturally responsive. Further, it requires that we examine the impact that our behaviors have on others.

- *"What do we need to begin?"* This question focuses groups or individuals on environmental factors that would support action, such as basic physical surroundings, tools, materials, supplies, and technology. To initiate change—to build equity—we have to identify our starting places.

Creating a Welcoming Climate

There is an old saying that the last thing a fish notices is the water it swims in, and this is true of the adults in a school when it comes to perceiving organizational culture. You've undoubtedly experienced this when you have entered a school that is unfamiliar to you. You're much more aware of the sights and sounds in this new place than you are in your current school.

Quickly, a definition, courtesy of the National School Climate Center (n.d.):

> School climate refers to the quality and character of school life. School climate is based on patterns of students', parents', and school personnel's experience of school life and reflects norms, goals, values, interpersonal relationships, teaching and learning practices, and organizational structures. (para. 3)

In other words, the school culture represents what a school collectively *does*, and the school's climate captures how the experience of being in that school *feels*. When a school's stated rules and norms are not aligned with what really occurs in hallways and classrooms, the school's climate suffers, and so do the individual relationships that teachers are building with their students. This misalignment sends the message that the rules are applied unevenly (perhaps even unfairly), leading students to feel that the relationships aren't trustworthy, either.

The district in which Pin Oak Elementary is located figured that families new to a school would be great at noticing the school's climate. They adapted a survey instrument (see Figure 2.1) and now send it out to families 30 days after a child's initial enrollment, translated into the family's home language as needed. Survey data are regularly compiled and shared with school leadership teams so that they can take action on feedback. Pin Oak principal Tate Jackson said, "I can tell you that a few years ago, the potential uses of this kind of feedback wasn't on my radar at all. Once we got students enrolled, made sure they were vaccinated, and got all the school records completed, we didn't intentionally interact with new families. Oh, sure, the ones that came to school got face time, but if we didn't see them, and there wasn't a problem with the child, we didn't really contact them personally."

Mr. Jackson knows that families have critical input to share, particularly in terms of how attached or connected to the school they feel. Consider that a child's strongest affiliation is usually with his or her family. When families experience a sense of "belonging to" a school, they transmit powerful messages to their children about education's importance in their lives. They influence their children in ways that align with the goals of schooling, and become a school's best allies when their children are struggling behaviorally or academically. Of course, building bonds with families is only one part of the equation. The relationships we build with students each day are what nourish the social-emotional engagement they require to succeed.

Relationships

Many studies have clearly linked positive student-teacher relationships to academic achievement. Hattie's (2012) analysis of the effect of positive student-teacher relationships on learning revealed an effect size of 0.72, equivalent to nearly two years of growth.

Teacher and administrator preparation programs stress the importance of positive student-teacher relationships, recognizing their accelerating effect on learning, and most school improvement plans call for taking steps to strengthen teacher-student relationships. This is easier said than done, however, owing to time constraints, cultural differences between teachers and students, and teachers' lack of experience with building these relationships.

FIGURE 2.1
New Family Survey

We would like to know your opinions on how well our school is meeting your family's and child(ren)'s needs and how you feel about your school experience.

- There are no right or wrong answers. We are interested only in your opinions.
- Your answers will be kept private. Your answers will be combined with those of other parents in a report of the survey findings.
- Your input is very important. Findings of the survey will be summarized and used to improve the school's efforts in strengthening the partnership between parents and the school.

What is/are your child(ren)'s grade level(s)? (circle all that apply)

K 1 2 3 4 5 6 7 8 9 10 11 12

Were any of these children enrolled at our school last year?   ☐ Yes   ☐ No

When you visit the school...	ALL of the time	MOST of the time	SOME of the time	NONE of the time
Is the reception staff friendly and helpful?				
Are the teachers easy to talk to?				
Are the administrators easy to talk to?				
Do you feel welcomed?				

What is/are the best way(s) to communicate with you and/or your family?
(choose all that apply)

☐ School memos (e-mails, website, letters, etc.)
☐ Children's teachers
☐ Counselor
☐ Direct contact (phone call, school/home visit, meeting)
☐ Other—please specify: _____

What else would you like to tell us about communication at our school? _____
_____
_____

Last school year, were you contacted by someone from the school regarding... (choose all that apply)

☐ Your child's academic success

☐ Your child's academic struggles

☐ Your child's positive social behavior

☐ Your child's negative social behavior

☐ Your child's recognition in achievement (sports, music, volunteerism, etc.)

☐ No reason, just to make contact (say hello, introduce self, etc.)

☐ Other—please specify: _____

What else would you like to tell us about contact regarding your child's successes and difficulties?

_____

_____

How much do you agree or disagree with the following statements?	STRONGLY agree	AGREE	DISAGREE	STRONGLY disagree
The school has high expectations for my child.				
The school clearly communicates those expectations to me and my child(ren).				
My child is learning what he or she needs to know to be successful after graduating.				
My child receives assistance when he or she is having difficulty academically or socially.				
The curriculum and activities keep my child interested and motivated.				
My child is happy at school.				

What else would you like to tell us about our school? _____

_____

_____

Thank you for taking the time to complete this survey. We can't be the Best School in the Universe without families like yours.

Source: Adapted from *How to Create a Culture of Achievement in Your School and Classroom* (pp. 181–182), by D. Fisher, N. Frey, and I. Pumpian, 2012, Alexandria, VA: ASCD. Copyright 2012 by ASCD.

To put it plainly, how does a teacher go about forging these more positive relationships?

Research tells us to that the key is for teachers to engage in caring behaviors—ones that provide emotional support, improved classroom organization, and instructional support (Allen et al., 2013). The behaviors associated with emotional support include those that demonstrate warmth and human connection, sensitivity to a student's academic and emotional states, and a regard for the child's opinions and perspectives. The behaviors associated with classroom organization and instructional support are the focus of Chapter 4, and we will explore them there. Here, we want to dig into emotional support.

Although kinds of behaviors may come more naturally to some than to others, they can be practiced and cultivated. When thinking about how teachers might become "more caring"—or, to put it clinically, habitually exhibit caring behaviors—it's helpful to reference the work of Purkey and Stanley (1991) and their concept of *invitational education.* They assert that there are four kinds of teachers: (1) intentionally inviting, (2) unintentionally inviting, (3) unintentionally uninviting, and (4) intentionally uninviting. We suggest that intentionally uninviting teachers should probably receive career counseling, as teaching clearly makes them deeply unhappy. The other three kinds of teachers merit a bit more discussion, though, as you can probably find yourself and nearly everyone in your building in these descriptions (see Figure 2.2):

- **Intentionally inviting teachers** actively seek to build connections each day with their students. They are purposeful in their actions, and demonstrate a belief in their students' ability to learn.
- **Unintentionally inviting teachers** are enthusiastic but not self-aware. These teachers may be newer to the profession and may be more tolerant of negative behavior from students. When things go awry, they are more vulnerable to hurt feelings.
- **Unintentionally uninviting teachers** signal their low expectations for their students and often possess a low sense of efficacy themselves. They want to do well but can't figure out how to turn the corner.

FIGURE 2.2
Invitational Teaching

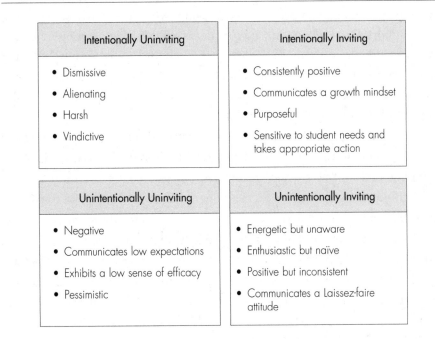

Intentionally Uninviting	Intentionally Inviting
• Dismissive • Alienating • Harsh • Vindictive	• Consistently positive • Communicates a growth mindset • Purposeful • Sensitive to student needs and takes appropriate action
Unintentionally Uninviting	**Unintentionally Inviting**
• Negative • Communicates low expectations • Exhibits a low sense of efficacy • Pessimistic	• Energetic but unaware • Enthusiastic but naïve • Positive but inconsistent • Communicates a Laissez-faire attitude

Source: Adapted from *Better Than Carrots or Sticks: Restorative Practices for Positive Classroom Management* (p. 23), by D. Smith, D. Fisher, and N. Frey, 2015, Alexandria, VA: ASCD. Copyright 2015 by ASCD.

Building relationships with students is hard work and requires daily reinvestment. Students need to be able to trust the consistency of the classroom environment, which stabilizes learning. Like all young people, they crave respect that is unconditional, and reward the respect they receive from adults by turning that respect toward others. Young people thrive in a climate that acknowledges reality but is optimistic overall. Obviously, building relationships with students is far more involved than heeding the standard "positive classroom management advice" to learn students' names, teach them the rules and norms, and demonstrate procedures. These steps, all associated with the beginning of the school year, certainly have value, but what about February? What about that Thursday afternoon when you don't feel well, or have a child of your own who may be coming down with something, and you've still got to go to the grocery store if there's going to be dinner tonight? Simply said, teacher actions during times of stress and worry are also noticed by students and can compromise relationships. Highly effective schools provide support for teachers, not just students—although this support comes back to students in the end. We titled this section "Relationships" because taking care of the adults in the school builds their capacity to take care of their students. Schools need to be not only the best places to learn but also the best places to teach and to work.

The relationships that students, teachers, and families build are tested when behavioral problems arise. Too often, the first time a discussion about discipline takes place is when an incident has created a crisis and emotions are high—a situation that leaves everyone involved less equipped to address the situation in a constructive way. This might explain why so many schools have relied on a system that prescribes specific disciplinary sanctions (like an automatic suspension) for specific offenses; it's a means of removing the family and the teacher from the equation. But this approach has earned deserved criticism for what it does to school communities in general and to certain groups of students in particular. Efforts to develop an alternative—and more equitable—approach to discipline have focused on restorative practices.

Restorative Practices

The statistics are incontrovertible: African American students, Hispanic/Latino students, students with disabilities, and linguistically diverse students are suspended and expelled at a disproportionate rate (U.S. Department of Education Office for Civil Rights, 2016). Students who are repeatedly suspended (the so-called "frequent flyers" who are suspended at least once per year) are more likely to drop out of school when they reach age 16 (Balfanz, Byrnes, & Fox, 2013). And why wouldn't they? The message they have received, over and over, is that they are "bad," that their behavior is shameful, that they don't deserve to be in class, and that if banishing them from class means they'll fall further behind academically, so be it. If you think about it, many "frequent flyers" make the most logical decision available to them: to leave school permanently. The unintended outcome of the zero-tolerance behavior policies that took root in the 1990s is generations of students who have been excluded from education. There has been a toll on communities as well. As suspension and expulsion rates have skyrocketed, tripling from 1973 to 2010 (Kennedy-Lewis & Murphy, 2016), the neighborhoods these students live in have deteriorated.

The phrase *restorative practices* is a nod to the approach's origins in *restorative justice*, which holds that punitive measures are an insufficient response to crime, and that offenders, especially young ones, should face their communities and endeavor to repair harm they have caused. A restorative justice perspective gives voice to those who have been affected and allows the offender to rebuild damaged relationships. A meta-analysis of a restorative justice approach with offenders found lower rates of recidivism and higher levels of victim satisfaction and restitution compliance compared to traditional adjudication (Latimer, Dowden, & Muise, 2005).

Restorative practices and social-emotional learning

The restorative practices approach includes requiring those who violate school rules to make reparations, but it's perhaps more notable for the way in which it focuses on proactively building the social-emotional capacity of students. The focus of the restorative practices work becomes learning new behaviors rather than simply punishing past behavior, and students' motivation to choose new behaviors comes from valuing and strengthening positive relationships. Although restorative justice–style victim-offender dialogue constitutes peacemaking efforts, a larger portion of attention is on the peace building that promotes communication among students and teachers (Smith, et al., 2015). The fundamental premise of restorative practices is that people are happier, more cooperative and productive, and more likely to make positive changes when those in positions of authority do things *with* them, rather than *to* them or *for* them (Costello, Watchel, & Wachtel, 2009). The following peace-building practices can be used every day in every classroom, in order to build relationships and deepen students' social-emotional learning.

Affective statements and questions. Affective statements and questions—expressing a message using an "I" statement—are fundamental peace-building tools. They are a simple way for any teacher to begin building relationships with students in that they convey the message, "I am talking with you, not at you." A teacher who responds to a behavioral issue with an "I" statement or question is clearly using his or her voice without co-opting the voice of the student. It's a way to communicate that you, the teacher, are not hurt by or frustrated with the student; rather, you are hurt by or frustrated with the actions he or she has taken, and you want to clarify your expectations and support different choices. For example, when a student is not engaged or is off task in class, a typical response might be to tell that student to pay attention. Now, contrast "Pay attention!" with the affective statement approach: "Tim, I'm disappointed that you are not paying attention. I feel like you could be more engaged in this assignment. That's not the Tim I know. How can I help you?" Which is more likely to result in Tim paying attention and engaging with the material?

We want to call out the importance of the last part of this affective statement, which sets it apart from a traditional redirect. Simply voicing disappointment isn't likely to result in anything more than a temporary change in Tim's behavior. But adding a statement about the child's identity ("That's not the Tim I know") followed by one that draws on his sense of agency ("How can I help you?") is caring behavior that lays the groundwork for an improved teacher-student relationship and better learning. Getting Tim to pay attention to this lesson is the short-term goal, but getting Tim more engaged in all lessons is the long game. Affective statements and questions support both.

Impromptu conversations. These short but informative private discussions are an effective way address the minor dust-ups that happen in the classroom all the time. Beneficial to both the adult and the student, they are typically used to resolve low-level problems before they get bigger, by prompting reflective thinking. When impromptu conversations are part of the classroom management toolkit, students don't get sent to the office for minor incidents and don't miss instruction.

Asking teachers to identify the number of impromptu conversations they have in a given week is an excellent way to assess a school's capacity to respond in a restorative way. It provides insight into the staff's capacity to act proactively and preventatively. As our experience demonstrates, and published research (e.g., Ingraham et al., 2016) confirms, as educators increase their use of restorative approaches, suspension rates will decline and fewer students will be sent out of class and miss part of their education. Other benefits of these impromptu conversations are that they help students learn what appropriate behavior is and allow teachers more autonomy to address situations within their classroom.

Circles. This well-known process in restorative practices allows students and teachers to hear one another as they work to find solutions to things that are disrupting learning. The process gets its name from its physical set-up. Chairs are generally arranged in a circle so that each member of the group can see everyone else, and obstructions, such as tables or desks, are moved out of the way. Teachers typically appreciate circles because they come with a set of ground rules that support civil discussion and provide a forum for discussing topics that are usually obvious but unstated. For example, Marco Ramirez used a circle when he observed one of his 3rd grade students teasing a new student at recess. Marcia Van Landingham used a circle to address her students' study habits in advance of their biology exam. Circles can and should be used for nonbehavioral reasons as well, such as discussing the ethics of medical testing on animals in biology class or how everyone is feeling about the upcoming test in a math class. We learned early on that it was important to use circles for content conversations as well as for behavior conversations when we realized that any time a group was asked to get in a circle, students immediately assumed someone was in trouble.

There are three types of circles: nonsequential, sequential, and fishbowl. In a *nonsequential circle*, a "talking piece" is issued, and only the person holding it can speak. This is a way to keep the conversation focused and orderly and to ensure that individual voices are heard. When a speaker has finished, he or she passes the talking piece to another member of the circle who has raised a hand to volunteer a comment or ask a question.

Sequential circles are used when you want to make sure every member of the group will participate in the conversation. The talking piece is passed sequentially around the circle, although the person holding it can opt to pass it on without comment. Low-stakes sequential circles can be used to help a class get to know and create connections with one another, and they can build trust for times when the group needs to talk about a much more complex or controversial issue. Topics of discussion for low-stakes sequential circles might include

- If you could be an animal, what kind would you be? Why?
- If you were a flavor of ice cream, what flavor would you be, and why?
- What is your dream vacation?
- What is the one word that best describes you?
- If you were stuck on a desert island, what one thing would you want?
- What is the story of your name?

Now, let's consider one of the more serious applications of a sequential circle: for resolving problems in the classroom. At the end of the school day, a teacher we know noticed that her desk drawer was open. When she walked over to close it, she saw that her bag had been rummaged through and that her phone was missing. Because her school uses restorative practices, she contacted an administrator to facilitate circles in her classes the following day. As the victim, she knew she should not attempt to objectively run the discussion. In each class period, once the students had gathered in a circle, the teacher shared that her smartphone contained the last photos she'd taken of her father, who had recently passed away. Then, the facilitator kicked off the discussion with a question: "What does a safe classroom feel like to you?" This question was a way to make the conversation about everyone in the classroom, not just the teacher. The students passed the talking piece around the circle and shared their responses. After each person had spoken, the facilitator reported what had happened the day before, and then helped each class process what had happened and how it felt to know this had occurred. The facilitator asked several questions, including these: *"What should be done when people experience a loss that threatens their sense of well-being?" "How can we repair the harm that has been done?" "Who can we ask to correct this situation, including returning the phone?"* He ended each circle by saying that if anyone knew the whereabouts of this missing phone, they could return it anonymously. The phone reappeared soon after dismissal.

Not all problems like this are resolved with circles, but a few things about this particular series of circles is important to note. The first is that the students were not treated like criminals. The facilitator kept the discussion focused on the harm done to the relationships within the classroom. After all, when a teacher's belongings go missing, everyone's property is at risk. The second is that the person who took the phone was probably moved to return it because he or she got to hear and see the damage taking it had done. And third—perhaps most important of all—the students wouldn't have cared about the pain this had caused their teacher or how the theft had undercut the shared trust in their classroom unless they already knew their teacher cared about them and they already cared about their classroom. Restorative practices focus on the violation of relationships, not rules. If there are no relationships, restorative practices won't work.

Fishbowl circles are similar to those used in Socratic seminars, with a circle within a circle. Members of the outside circle witness what the inner circle is discussing. The optimal way to conduct a fishbowl circle is to leave an empty chair or two in the inner circle so that people from the outer circle can jump in to participate at particular points. After the inner circle finishes its discussion, those students move to the outer circle, and the outer-circle listeners take their place in the "fishbowl." The new inner circle continues the discussion, restating what they heard.

At the school where we work, 8th graders held a fishbowl after tensions broke out between the boys and the girls in the class. Students took a place in the inner or outer circles based on their gender: boys together and girls together. In the fishbowl, the girls talked about body image issues while the boys listened. When they traded places, the boys first repeated what they believed they heard, and then shared their own concerns about the expectations they felt to "be a man." Next, the girls went back to the inner circle and repeated the concerns the boys had listed. At this point, the facilitator, a 7th grade teacher, had the whole class reconfigure into a nonsequential circle, where they discussed actions and language they could use to reduce one another's anxieties.

The social-emotional learning that comes from restorative practices is not primarily about solving victim-offender transgressions. Although these receive more attention due to their higher profile, the real work, and the real payoff, comes from building the communication, self-regulation, and reflective thinking skills of all the students in the school. It's generally true that most of the challenging discipline problems are concentrated among a small percentage of the student body. Restorative practices are designed to help them, of course, but also to extend the benefits to all students by promoting a proactive and preventative mindset. We've seen firsthand the effects that children and adolescents trained in restorative practices can have over time in their own families and communities. Communicative, self-regulating, and reflective young people are exactly what our society needs.

Attendance

Students are absent from school for a variety of reasons, including health problems, childcare issues, doctor appointments, and family trips. But chronic absenteeism, defined as missing at least 10 percent of the school year (18 days in most states) is an issue apart—an area that affects student achievement. That effect is magnified for students living in poverty. Estimates are that somewhere between 10 and 12.5 percent of U.S. students and between 5 and 7.5 million children nationwide have chronic attendance problems (Balfanz & Byrnes, 2012). Missing two or three days a month adds up quickly and has lasting effect on learning (Allensworth & Easton, 2007; Balfanz & Byrnes, 2012). Consider the following:

- Third graders who are chronically absent are less likely to read at grade level.
- Chronic absenteeism in 6th grade is a strong predictor of dropping out in high school.

- Ninth grade attendance is a better predictor of achievement than 8th grade test scores.

We have saved this important issue of chronic absenteeism for the end of this section because we want to stress how fostering a culturally proficient and welcoming climate and a restorative environment can combat it. Attendance rates are evidence of the attachment students have to their school and the people who work and learn there. Think of it as students voting with their feet; when they choose not to be in school, it's feedback about school's status in their lives. The relationships educators build and maintain with students and their families make school feel like a valuable place. They are what make children feel that they are cared for at school and missed when they are absent.

The attendance clerk at the school where we work helps us by sending a list each morning of the names of students present that day who were absent the day before. With this list, we can say to individual students, "I'm glad you're back. I missed you yesterday." Home visits are another way our school responds to absenteeism. There might be an issue with transportation—perhaps the family doesn't feel their child is safe walking to and from school. Or there might be some underlying mental or physical health issues within the home that are contributing to the number of absences. The social worker and special educators at the school where we work are the ones who most frequently make home visits. They report that in many cases it's a matter of educating the caregiver. "It's surprising how often parents think that as long as the absence is excused, it somehow doesn't count," said one. This is a common misconception about absences. Providing families with information on the negative effects of absenteeism can influence choices they make about childcare, vacations, and even weather conditions.

This brings us back to restorative practices and the need to align our school culture with the climate we hope to create. Knowing the negative effects of chronic absenteeism, why would educators contribute to it by routinely suspending students from their education? A day away from the classroom matters, regardless of the reason. A statistic from earlier in this chapter bears repeating: students suspended at least once per year are more likely to drop out of school when they reach age 16 (Balfanz, et al., 2013). The great irony is that a national study conducted in 2015 found that schools with higher percentages of black students are less likely to use restorative practices, and instead use punitive disciplinary measures at higher rates (Payne & Welch, 2015). And we know that dropout rates are higher in schools with higher concentrations of students living in poverty as well as in schools that have higher percentages of students of color (see, for example, Riddle, 2013). Given that schools with higher percentages of traditionally under-represented students use restorative practices less frequently, is it possible that their more punitive actions increase absenteeism and contribute to the dropout problem?

The peacemaking efforts used in schools can reduce the number of suspensions and therefore the number of absences. But perhaps most effective of all are the relationship-building practices educators engage in each day: the brief conversations that build a student's agency and identity along with the intentionally inviting instruction that helps all students understand that they are a vital part of the classroom community. When students know how much you care, they begin to care about how much you know and begin to want to let you in.

Response to Trauma

Ninth grade math teacher Tim Duncan watches Derek drop his skateboard outside the front door of Lexington Charter and disappear across the corner. Mr. Duncan leans over to Alice Farrell, the 9th grade English teacher, and comments, "I just don't get much out of that kid." To which Ms. Farrell responds, "Me either. See you tomorrow." The conversation ends there, but the story itself has everlasting consequences.

Derek has one dead parent and one parent in jail, and there is strong inference that the death and the incarceration are directly connected. Just what *do* Mr. Duncan and Ms. Farrell expect to get out of Derek this year? If this is the first and only question we ask, the answer is an obvious one: they will get very little learning from him and probably lots of problematic behavior and underachievement. Here's a better question to ask: *What should Derek expect from his teachers this year?*

Derek should expect from them the awareness that trauma has rocked the very foundation of his mental health and well-being, and that this trauma is compromising his performance as a capable, engaged student. He should expect his teachers, along with the rest of the school leadership, staff, and community to help him counteract the ways that trauma is literally rewiring his brain (van der Kolk, 2014). Derek should also expect the members of his school community to be prepared to take this action because they realize his trauma, however profound, is hardly an anomaly.

The number of children in our schools exposed to traumatic events is staggering. Results from the National Survey of Children's Health indicate that almost half of U.S. public school students have experienced at least one serious trauma and a third of students between the ages of 12 and 17 have experienced two or more traumatic events likely to affect their physical and mental well-being (Stevens, 2012). Imagine 35 million children in our schools who have witnessed family violence or have been physically or sexually abused and neglected. The National Institutes of Health (2016) reports on its website that "just over 20 percent (or 1 in 5) children, either currently or at some point during their life, have had a seriously debilitating mental disorder" (para. 1).

How dare we let another generation of Mr. Duncans and Ms. Farrells simply wonder *what they can expect to get from their Dereks?* There is no equity in keeping ourselves unaware and insensitive to the huge number of children who should expect their schools to be aware, sensitive, and responsive to their mental health and well-being. Our failure to do this compromises the very foundation of our educational missions and every other initiative to provide more students the quality educational programs and outcomes we all value. Children affected by toxic trauma wander through school in fight, flight, or freeze mode (Stevens, 2012), ill-prepared to take advantage of our curriculum or instruction.

As school leaders have become more aware of and sensitive to these alarming statistics and their human and educational implications, new policies and programs are taking shape. States, districts, and individual schools and communities are rallying to create schoolwide practices that are directly informed by what we know about trauma-sensitive approaches designed to help students feel academically, socially, emotionally, and physically safe (Stevens, 2012), which is essential to increasing their school engagement and learning. These practices also ensure, through direct services and partnerships with other agencies, that counseling and social work services therapeutically wrap around the school in general and around specific students in particular. Building caring and trusting relationships will help students feel that school is a safe place to open up and succeed. Being aware of and sensitive to factors that affect the mental health and well-being of our students will help us choose schoolwide practices that will be responsive to student needs. We offer the Building Equity Review as one means to generate better information on the limitations of current practices so that better, more responsive practices can be explored and implemented. Those responsive practices are essential elements of any school's evolving plan for greater equity.

Building Equity Review Statements: Social-Emotional Engagement

The five statements in this section focus on the social and emotional support that teachers can provide for their students. We discuss them and then examine the ways in which specific schools have addressed the equity gaps that consideration of these statements can bring to light.

6. The social and emotional needs of students are adequately supported in the school, from prosocial skills development to responsiveness to trauma.

To create an equitable school, teachers and other staff members have to recognize the social and emotional needs within their student population and then identify ways to meet those needs. Failure to do so places some students at increased risk and furthers—or even creates—inequities that are difficult to overcome.

We recognize that all students present social and emotional needs that should be addressed by schoolwide structures, and that our student body includes some whose well-being and learning have already been compromised by major crises. School mental health professionals now commonly recognize the need to meet the full array of social and emotional needs through a three-tiered approach (Fazel, Hoagwood, Stephan, & Ford, 2014):

1. Universal mental health promotion for all students.
2. Selective services for students identified as at risk for a mental health concern or problem.
3. Indicated services for individual students who already display a mental health concern or problem.

This kind of tiered approach is a welcome alternative to random and fragmented programs and services, and it has been endorsed by such notable initiatives as the National Positive Behavioral Interventions & Supports Center (see Barrett, Eber, & Weist, 2009). As you consider evidence gathered through the Building Equity Review, you might consider using this tiered system to structure the discussions about how to better foster the social and emotional well-being of your student body.

That is what the staff at Washington Middle School did. As one of the teachers participating in the Building Equity Review noted while reading the responses to the question that heads this section, "We have a lot of students who lack social skills, and I don't think we've done much about that. We've been focused on their academics, and we've made progress. But it's clearly time we think about the social development of these young adolescents." The vast majority of participating teachers agreed and expressed support for an effort to help Washington students develop prosocial behaviors while at school. One of the more reluctant teachers commented on what had swayed her to this point of view: "I really don't think that this is our responsibility— it's their parents' job. But I've been thinking about this, and I believe what we do here could spill over into the rest of our students' lives, and the community would be better off for that. So I'm interested in hearing some ideas and seeing if we can make this happen."

The school formed an action group to make recommendations to the entire faculty about improving the social skills of the students. Following a few meetings, the action group had identified several practical places to start. They decided to do the following:

- **Teach social skills.** These included fundamentals like handshakes, culturally appropriate eye contact, visually tracking speakers, and incorporating "manners words" like *please* and *thank you.*
- **Focus schoolwide on *respect*.** The action team recommended a school assembly on the topic and developed a series of short lessons that could be implemented during homeroom to highlight what respectful interactions with peers and with adults look like. They even purchased inexpensive t-shirts with the word *respect* printed next to the school logo and name.
- **Reinvest in restorative practices.** Upon reflection, the action team realized that efforts to address lower levels of problematic behavior were slipping and that instances of discourteous behavior were being ignored. They requested time during several upcoming professional learning events to validate and extend teachers' skills in using impromptu conversations and circles.
- **Ensure an adequate and coordinated array of services to meet specific needs.** The action team knew specific students would require professional counseling and individualized social work services. They embraced the three-tiered approach, knowing that the schoolwide practices they were promoting needed to be supplemented with specialized professional services for an identified group of students with mental health needs. The team requested more clarity from the district office regarding referral procedures and also recommended new community partnerships with agencies that could provide therapeutic counseling and social work to supplement those available through the school system. Finally the team affirmed their commitment to communicate to all students that school was a safe place to be and to seek help.

The social-emotional action team at Washington Middle School also issued the strong recommendation that teachers modify their daily learning objectives to include clear social expectations. As one of the action team members commented, "We're really clear with students about what we want them to learn in terms of content and language, but we don't necessarily share our expectations for their social skills. It would be really easy to add social expectations to our lessons so that this is addressed every day, in every class." The teachers at Washington agreed and began to implement social learning targets in their classrooms (others call them *learning intentions, objectives,* or *goals*). This was not always easy; most teachers maintained some social learning targets focused on compliance (e.g., "Raise your hand before speaking"). Over time, however, teachers began to develop clearer and clearer expectations for students' social behavior and to set learning targets like these:

- Track the speaker with your eyes and body.
- Practice active listening techniques, such as nonverbal behaviors.
- Take turns talking, so that each member of the group has a chance to share.
- Invite group members who have not spoken to share their thinking.

Most significantly, the students started living up to these expectations. Twelve weeks after the initial meeting, the reluctant teacher we quoted earlier was overhead commenting that her class was "a different place now. It's not like all the kids behave perfectly," she said, "but there's a new level of respect for the learning environment, and when problems arise, there is language we can all use to redirect the issue. The social expectations that I establish help them learn new skills. It's just like the content I need for them to learn. And, with all of us doing this, the range of social skills that our students have mastered is impressive."

When the teachers at McQueen Elementary School examined their responses to this statement in the Building Equity Review, their discussion focused on a different concern—namely, the number of their students who had experienced trauma. The type of trauma varied: the loss of a close friend or family member, a serious injury or emergency, widespread disaster, violence, abuse, divorce, homelessness, bankruptcy, and a range of other issues. The severity of the trauma differed among students, too, but all those who had experienced trauma had some things in common, and chief among them was a tendency to revisit the traumatic event or events, whether that be in their writing, their nightmares, or their actions. Elementary school teacher Leanne Richardson wanted to know how to spot students who had experienced trauma, so she developed a quick checklist that her colleagues could use (see Figure 2.3).

Figure 2.3
Checklist of Warning Signs for Trauma

☐ Re-experiencing the event
- ○ Nightmares
- ○ Daytime distraction (lost in thought about the event)
- ○ Disturbing thoughts, feelings, words
- ○ Drawing pictures of the event or related to the event
- ○ Inability to concentrate
- ○ Loss of appetite (and possible weight loss)
- ○ Lower energy levels
- ○ Trouble sleeping

☐ Avoidance of traumatic reminders
- ○ Disinterest in daily activities
- ○ Generally withdrawn
- ○ Fearful or anxious
- ○ Chooses self-isolation
- ○ Hypersensitive and easily startled

☐ Regressive behavior
- ○ Cries easily
- ○ Sucks thumb
- ○ Carries a soothing object (like a stuffed animal)

- ○ Bathroom accidents
- ○ Bedwetting
- ○ Childish fears (e.g., monsters)
- ○ Speech problems

☐ Physical pain
- ○ Headaches
- ○ Stomachaches

☐ Irritability
- ○ Anger
- ○ Aggression
- ○ Resentfulness
- ○ Feelings of unfairness
- ○ Bitterness

☐ Memory problems
- ○ Difficulty remembering the traumatic event
- ○ Difficulty with general memory

☐ Extreme fearfulness
- ○ Overprotection of self
- ○ Overprotection of loved ones
- ○ New irrational fears

Source: Developed by Leanne Richardson. Used with permission.

As the staff at McQueen Elementary School began to address the needs of their students who had experienced trauma, they realized that several of the actions they identified as beneficial would require the involvement of the school counselor or social worker. They also realized that the counselor's or social worker's effectiveness could be enhanced by ensuring classroom teachers had clear plans for supporting students. Here are some of the ideas they generated.

Make the classroom as predictable as possible. For many students who have experienced trauma, unpredictable events are a trigger. They typically appreciate routines that they can count on and tend to do better when informed in advance that routines need to be changed.

Ensure that every student has a trusted adult on campus. As we have noted, student-teacher relationships are a powerful tool for students' learning. This is heightened in situations in which the student has experienced trauma. In some cases, a previously trusted adult caused the traumatic event(s), leading the student to have trouble developing relationships. Having said that, teachers who redouble their efforts to develop trusting relationships with students who have experienced trauma can help them heal.

Incorporate identity- and esteem-building activities. Having responsibilities and being trusted are things that all of us value. Students who have experienced trauma may feel that their identity has been compromised. Teachers can help these students rebuild their sense of self by changing the narrative that students tell about themselves. There are several books devoted entirely to this topic (e.g., Johnston, 2004), and they all recommend that teachers use language as a tool to help shape students' identity. For example, a teacher might say, "That's not the Matthew I know. The Matthew I know allows his friends to take a turn." In another situation, a teacher might say, "Jacqueline, I'm thinking of the different ways that writers share what they have in their minds. Sometimes they provide rich descriptions. That's what you did, right? Tell me more about the choices you've made to share your thinking." When students encounter adults who help them change the narrative they use to describe themselves, they begin to see themselves differently and can learn to heal from negative experiences they have had. We are not minimizing the role that professional counseling plays in helping students; we are emphasizing that teachers can be partners in this process.

Provide quiet time. For some students who have experienced trauma, having time each day to relax and settle their thoughts can be useful. We're not suggesting that students simply be given free time, and we recognize that unstructured time may be difficult for some students to manage and unwise for others. This approach is best taken when students have been taught meditation techniques by their counselors and need time to use those tools, or have been taught techniques for calming themselves, such as counting back from 25 or 50 or focusing on breathing.

7. Teachers and staff show they care about students.

Responding to this item on the Building Equity Review requires an examination of the actual behaviors of the adults in the school. Teachers who believe that they routinely demonstrate great care for students are often surprised to learn, post-observation, that they rarely exhibit demonstrably caring behaviors. The outward signs that teachers and staff use to show they care are diverse and often idiosyncratic, meaning that they are different for different people. Consider the following three examples:

- A teacher greets each student at the door with a handshake, high-five, or slight bow based on his relationship with each student who enters the room.
- A teacher writes personal notes in each student's writing journal, recognizing strengths and weaknesses, and making recommendations.
- A teacher regularly makes connections between her content and students' personal interests.

We share these examples because they are easy ways for adults to show that they care about students. We're not suggesting that every teacher adopt all of these but rather that they develop their own approach to showing students that they care about them—and, specifically, that they care about each student as an individual.

When the teachers at Carlos Riviera High School conducted a full Building Equity Audit and reviewed responses to the student survey (see Appendix B), they learned that many students at their school did not believe that their teachers cared about them. As one of the teachers noted, "We all rated ourselves highly on the care question, but the students did not. In fact, it's the biggest discrepancy on the whole audit. We *do* care about them, so let's figure out how to show them that we do!" Another teacher commented, "You're right that it's the biggest difference, but I just don't understand it. Maybe we should have some student focus groups and figure out if our definitions of care are the same." And this is exactly where the staff started. They invited a range of students to focus group meetings, and they served pizza to entice students to come. What the Riviera teachers learned changed their perspectives and their practices.

First and foremost, most students said that they believed that the teachers *liked* them but didn't really *care* about them. When asked to provide examples of how they knew teachers liked them, they shared lots of examples, including these:

- "You know all of our names, and you say hello to us."
- "You know stuff about most of us and what we like."
- "You try to know about things that we care about, such as Pokémon Go and Snapchat."
- "You smile a lot when you're at school."

Why did they say, then, that teachers didn't care about them?

- "You never go to our sports events, dances, or other things outside of school."
- "You don't give us a second chance when we don't do well in your class."

As the staff of Carlos Riviera High School noted, they needed to do a better job of demonstrate their caring in a way that students would *recognize* as caring, and now that they had a working definition, they could get started.

They agreed to develop a schedule of extracurricular events and identify different staff members who could attend each. As one of the teachers said, "It's in our contract to supervise events, but I go to the same ones each time, mostly because of my interests. For example, I've never gone to a play, even though I know that I have students in my classes who are into drama. I will commit to changing my supervisions around a bit so that students see me at different events." In fact, all of the teachers agreed to do this, not because it was required or requested by their principal but because they wanted their students to know that they were cared about.

To address the second sign of caring the students had identified, the giving of second chances, the Riviera faculty decided to review syllabi. What they found—that there generally were no options to retake exams or redo projects or essays—backed up students' conclusion that their teachers didn't care. This raised a lot of issues for discussion. Some teachers thought that students wouldn't try hard enough on the first attempt if they knew that they would have a second chance. Others worried about the increased workload if lots of students wanted to redo work. They put off making a decision, but the issue plagued a group of teachers in the English department, who continued the discussion on their own.

"It's not like our kids will be able to redo or make up work in college," one said. "Isn't it our responsibility to make sure they learn that now?" Another chimed in, "I hear you, but then I think about students who really want to learn our content and might master it if given another chance." Then a third teacher said this:

> I hear you both, but I'm thinking that this is an equity issue. The students who mainly get good scores on essays and assessments always get good scores. I think I could level the playing field for the ones who struggle more by making sure they have the opportunity to learn from their errors and make improvements. I'm thinking that I'll make two or three versions of the test, and if they want to try again after seeing how they performed, I'll allow it. And if they meet with me to talk through their essay and my feedback, and then they rewrite it, I'm going to grade it again. I want to see if this practice will change the outcomes of our students' experience. Their saying

that we don't care about them really hit me. I've had a lot of second chances, sometimes even more chances. I want students to know that I care, and if this helps, I'm all for it. But I also want them to learn to write and analyze texts. So if it takes a little longer for some students, then I'm OK with that.

And there it was. These comments, from a veteran teacher, changed the dynamics of the department's approach. They moved to mastery, or competency-based, grading, providing students with structured opportunities to try again. Some students immediately took advantage of the opportunities, and others had to be encouraged to do so. The results speak for themselves. The overall grade point average in English classes increased, as did student performance on state tests. And students started talking about how much their English teachers cared about their learning, so much so that the math teachers decided to change their practices the following semester, and the rest of the teachers in the school revised their grading policies the following school year. The teachers at Carlos Riviera High School used the data they gathered from the Building Equity Audit to make decisions that improved the school experience for everyone and ensured that students who needed something extra in order to be "equal" received it.

8. *The school has programs and policies that are designed to improve attendance.*

School attendance is like the warning lights on the dashboards of our vehicles. Sometimes, you need to take immediate action, and other times you can wait. But the light is telling you something, and you do need to pay attention.

The staff at Jefferson Middle School noted that there was a group of students who were chronically absent, meaning that they missed more than 10 percent of the school year. Until the Jefferson faculty and staff completed the Building Equity Audit, they hadn't really paid attention to this group of students and had focused instead on those who missed a lot more school, upward of 40 or 50 percent. The school had put sophisticated plans in place to address the needs of students in this situation, including an early warning system from their feeder elementary schools, a teacher who provided instruction at home for students with chronic health challenges, and a social worker who was available to meet with families to develop systems of support, including behavioral interventions to address students' actions at home.

Prompted by their audit data to take a closer look at attendance, a team of Jefferson faculty saw that there was a portion of students who were still missing a significant number of days—10 to 20 percent of the year—but not being reached by the existing programs and policies. They saw that these absences were largely excused by parents, and that it was rare for the students to miss two days in a row. They decided to interview the parents to learn more about the issues that prevented students from attending school. To their surprise, more than half of the students in this group had disabilities. Their parents reported that students said that they "just didn't feel well" and had asked to stay home. As one parent said, "It's not that he was super sick or anything."

Digging a little deeper, the team started talking with this cohort of students about their absences and learned that they often stayed home when they thought that they would be bullied or if they had been a victim of bullying the day before. No, they had not reported these incidents or fears, they confessed. They had not felt comfortable enough to do so, or they were embarrassed.

This is how inquiring into absenteeism triggered Jefferson Middle School's widespread campaign to address a bullying problem that the staff had not been aware of. The principal made it clear that bullying would not be tolerated. He held a series of parent meetings to talk about victims, bystanders, and bullies. The staff collected student-generated data on bullying and other dangerous situations through the anonymous reporting system Sprigeo (http://sprigeo.com). They also enlisted the help of the elected student government group and the school TV station to focus on bullying prevention efforts. Soon there were posters around the school making it clear that bullying was not cool and that it was in the best interest of everyone to tell a trusted adult when anyone was bullied.

Unsurprisingly, the number of bullying reports increased dramatically. There were reports of bullying almost every other day. Some were not serious, or even bullying, but some were. And true to his word, the principal investigated each case and worked to resolve each situation, often with restorative practices but sometimes through parent meetings and community service. Over time, the number of reports dropped off, and the group of students who had been missing school were nearly always present. As is often the case, this attendance issue was an indicator of an equity issue that the individuals within the school could address.

9. The school's discipline plans are restorative rather than punitive.

In defiance of reality, which is seldom black and white, we framed this item in the Building Equity Review as a stark dichotomy—an either/or choice of whether a school's discipline plans are restorative or punitive. It's a way to force consideration of the ways in which the harm that occurs within a school is repaired, and if harm is repaired at all.

As we have discussed, restorative approaches to problematic behavior and actions allow students (and staff) to learn from the mistakes they've made and move on, having learned that lesson. We also recognize that there are times when restorative practices won't work, such as when someone refuses to participate in the conversation, or when the victim can't forgive, or when the perpetrator has no remorse. Often, these cases just need more time, and restoration will come later. But some situations are more stubborn, and students refuse to restore. In those cases, punitive approaches may be the last resort. This particular item in the BER asks for a judgment specifically related to the ways in which students are treated when they are still learning to behave.

We have had students over the years make terrible decisions when dealing with their own personal feelings, and we have come to understand the degree to which their reactions are influenced by the world around them, including the adult and peer models they see. In addition, students react in a wide range of ways to situations in which they feel powerless or voiceless—when they don't get their way, feel harmed, or are embarrassed or hurt. For example, students in elementary grades might have a tantrum, throw objects, kick and scream, or use foul language. In upper grades, especially in high school, students tend to remove themselves from school, fight, attack others verbally, or self-medicate. The challenge is that educators must learn to understand that there are obstacles in every child's life and that they are often the "first responders" when these outbursts happen. The triage they provide is powerful.

Let's consider Abdu, for example. He is a bright young man who entered our school in 7th grade after having struggled in previous schools and being removed from one school after another. His older brother had experienced success at our school, so Abdu came to us. He was opposed to this. He didn't want to know staff or build relationships with anybody. He wanted to do his own thing, his own way.

A few days after enrolling, Abdu decided to pull the fire alarm inside our building, sending the entire school into evacuation mode and automatically alerting the fire department. When we found out Abdu had done this, Dominique, an administrator, met with him to have a conversation. The first thing Abdu said was, "How long am I suspended?" This caught Dominique by surprise; he was not used to having this kind of conversation include talk of suspension.

He paused just a moment, then asked Abdu, "How do you like the school?" Now it was Abdu's turn to be surprised. "What do you mean, 'how do I like school'?" he shot back. Dominique persisted. "How do you like this school?" he asked. Abdu gave a typical 7th grader's response: "It's cool, I guess." But the questions from Dominique continued: "Why did you choose this school?" "What class have you enjoyed the most?" "How has your day been today?"

It was clear that Abdu was starting to feel confused, because there had been no questions about the fire alarm, but he answered the questions put to him. He'd gotten in trouble and his parents had chosen this school, not him. He enjoyed history the best. His day was bad.

Dominique saw an opportunity he'd been looking for. "Why is your day bad?" he asked. Again, Abdu looked up with confusion. "It's bad because my dad left and isn't coming home for six months," he said. The tough 7th grader had let his mask slip a little, giving his administrator a look at the hurt kid behind it.

"I'm sorry that you're hurting," Dominque said. "Did that play into the situation today?" Abdu looked up again, realizing that finally, here was the fire alarm question he'd been expecting. "Yeah," he said. "I wanted to get caught. I wanted you to call home. I wanted to talk to my dad, and I knew my mom would call him if I got in trouble."

The conversation continued from there. Dominique went on to inform Abdu that the decision he'd made wasn't a smart one and wasn't his best choice. He added that he understood Abdu was just trying to be heard, trying to use his voice. "If you want to talk to your dad, Abdu, I'll figure out a way to help."

"Are you calling my mom?" Abdu asked. Dominique replied that he wouldn't, because he didn't want his first conversation with Abdu's mother to be a negative one. He then explained that he wanted Abdu to be able to own this poor choice and to make things right with his classmates. Abdu agreed and said he wanted to apologize to each class and be able to move forward. Dominique agreed to help him make these apologies. As they walked out of the office, Abdu stopped, looked at Dominique and said, "Thanks. No one has ever heard my voice before."

This is one example of how an administrator took the time to build a relationship with a student. The entire point of the exchange was to get Abdu back into a learning environment and keep the problematic behavior from happening again. The next day, Abdu's mother came to school. She was very apologetic, saying, "I'll pay the fine for the false fire alarm, and you can suspend him, but please don't kick him out of your school. It's the first time that *he* came to tell me what he did wrong instead of it being the school or police." Not only did Abdu confess responsibility to his mom, he also carried through with his plan of asking forgiveness from every class for interrupting their learning.

It's been several years since that fire alarm was pulled, and Abdu has come a long way. He's still a work in progress, and he is often distracted and distracting in class. His dad did not come back; instead, he sent Abdu photos of himself with a new wife and child. Despite ongoing issues with anger and abandonment, Abdu has never caused another major incident at our school.

Instead, he has passed all of his classes and has found a place for himself. He's on track to graduate and has ambitions to join the Coast Guard. Now take a moment to imagine where Abdu might be now if our school's discipline plans had been punitive rather than restorative.

10. *Students are treated equitably when they misbehave, and consequences are based on an ethic of care rather than demographic characteristics.*

When problematic behavior occurs, teachers, parents, and administrators have to respond. How we respond, and whether or not we respond in an equitable way, matters a great deal.

We caution against using a cookie-cutter approach to discipline and applying the same consequences to every situation. It may seem "fair" for all students to receive the same consequences for a particular offense regardless of the situation, its context, or students' ability to address or repair the harm done. All too often, however, this results in inequitable disciplinary practices because it fails to acknowledge students as complicated individuals with specific histories and challenges. Providing a wider range of actions and consequences makes it easier to notice when harsher (or more lenient) disciplinary actions are correlated with student demographics.

We believe that discipline should be based on an ethic of care. We're not suggesting that problematic behavior be ignored, nor are we "soft on crime." We simply believe in using caring relationships to ensure that students (and adults) know that their actions can cause harm. An ethic of care provides a foundation on which to build and fosters empathy and connection. It's about enlightenment, not punishment. It requires and motivates students who misbehave to repair the harm they have done to others and return the situation to normalcy as soon as possible.

Let's look at some approaches to discipline that would merit a "no" response to this item on the Building Equity Review. At Juarez Elementary, all problematic behaviors are treated the same, regardless of the cause or consequences. For example, any student who runs in the hallway experiences progressive disciplinary consequences. On the first offense, the student has to start over and walk the hallway the correct way. On the second offense, the student has to walk the hallway again and then write "I will not run in the hallway" 25 times. On the third offense, the student has to do all of above and practice walking in the hallway repeatedly (probably until the person supervising gets tired). On the fourth offense, the student has a meeting with the principal. This progression continues until the student is suspended.

The problem is that no one asks at any of these stages *why* the student is running. Would you entertain that running away from a bully is different than being silly? What about running because you have to go to the bathroom so badly that you can't hold it any longer? Or running because you're excited to see your dad for the first time in the six months since his deployment? Running is the infraction, but it's the reason for the running that is important. Yes, we want schools to be safe and not have students running wildly through the halls, but a conversation with a student in some of these situations might be all it takes to correct the problem and avoid any of the punishments listed.

Sometimes schools try to manage problematic behavior through application of peer pressure. Davis Middle School has a strict dress code; everyone wears a uniform. It also has a problem with students fighting. To address the fighting, the administration and staff made a deal with students: if no one in a given grade level fights for one week, all students in that grade level are allowed to wear street clothes to class rather than the required uniform.

It seems very strange to us to reward students for not breaking one rule by letting them break another rule, and misguided to send the message that wearing uniforms is a bad situation that students will naturally want to get out of. But most alarming, it suggests that there is no other system in place to control the fights on campus. When we asked for details of this policy, we learned that each grade level earns the right to not wear uniforms just once or twice per year. In other words, the vast majority of weeks there are fights, and it's clear that for some students, fighting is much more important than getting to wear street clothes at school. When we asked about the students who fight, we learned that there was a small group of students who fought regularly, but that nearly 75 percent of the students had been in a fight sometime during middle school. To our thinking, Davis's policy for addressing the problem of fights doesn't seem to be working.

In some schools, inequitable disciplinary practices are entrenched, meaning that specific groups of students are consistently singled out for discipline and receive a disproportionate amount of more severe consequences. This was the case at Adams High School, where black students were three times more likely to be suspended than white or Asian students who had committed the same offense. Latino/Hispanic students were twice as likely to be suspended as white or Asian students. Disciplinary consequences for all Adams athletes typically involved them having to sit out games; black athletes had to sit out more games than students of other races or ethnicities.

When Adams High School engaged in a Building Equity Review, the results suggested that race/ethnicity was affecting the decisions about discipline. As one of the leaders of the school noted, "The first step is to acknowledge that you have a problem, then you can go about addressing it." And that's what the team at Adams did. They acknowledged the problem and identified a number of potential solutions. They agreed to engage in restorative practices training. They invited a local expert to provide optional but compensated professional learning opportunities for teachers during their prep periods that focused on impromptu conversations. And they agreed to meet weekly as a team to present discipline cases and discuss consequences. As part of their equity planning, they went on to chart the disciplinary decisions made in order to flag disparities in their actions so that they could better identify the triggers that led them to treat students differently.

First Steps: It Starts with You

No one needs to wait for the school to make a decision to address the social-emotional learning of children and adolescents. Any adult, certificated or certified, can use a simple process called 2x10 (Wlodkowski, 1983). It works like this: every day for 10 school days, engage a student in a two-minute conversation that has nothing to do with academics. Ask her if she saw the last basketball game, or tell her about a movie you want to see over d 2 cool d

| perfect

Cessy

4*·c

0 8 4 22

$

Sept 4677

Sept 81

Moron

044,1110

4677

the weekend and inquire about her plans. Ask for a book recommendation for your nephew, who is the same age as the student. Consistency is key to the 2x10 process. These short but regular interactions are foundational to relationships, especially for those who might otherwise be overlooked. No need to put together a written plan. Just try it out, and see how your relationships with students change.

Conclusion

The academic lives of students can be dramatically affected by the social and emotional support they receive. Sometimes the effect is positive, and at other times it's negative. Our concern with equity compels us to pay special attention to providing positive support to our students who live in poverty, who have a history of behavioral struggles, who have experienced trauma, and who face discrimination for some aspect of their identity.

The good news is that schools, and the adults who work in them, can do this effectively. And when we do, equity becomes increasingly attainable. Like integration, social and emotional engagement is a necessary ingredient in the equity process. It's not sufficient in and of itself, but the absence of focused efforts to build students' social and emotional skills will certainly compromise efforts to ensure quality educational and life outcomes for students. A sustainable, positive school climate fosters youth development and learning necessary for a productive, contributing, and satisfying life in a democratic society.

CHAPTER 3

Opportunity to Learn
Just-in-Time Supports Meet More Needs

If you work in a school that serves a number of English learners, here is a scenario that is probably familiar to you.

The four kindergarten teachers at Capitol Park Elementary each have four or five students who have been classified as "English learners," meaning that the language spoken at these children's homes is different from the language spoken at school. Each of these kindergarten teachers has received training in the needs and characteristics of English learners and knows how to employ strategies such as using realia and incorporating Total Physical Response. But each of these teachers is using grouping differently in his or her mathematics instruction:

- Ms. Campbell combines whole-group instruction with small-group learning. She groups all her English learners together in a permanent homogenous small group so she "can give them specialized supports and instruction."
- Like his colleagues, Mr. Andrews also uses both whole-group and small-group learning in math. However, he employs heterogeneous grouping, placing a single English learner within each of the math groups "so that these kids get lots of exposure to native English speakers."
- Ms. Barnett also teaches math using both whole-group and small-group instruction. In addition, she strategically uses a combination

of heterogeneous and homogenous small-group instruction with her English learners. "There are times when I need to make sure they are getting specialized supports, like teaching them academic language structures, but there are other times when they benefit more from learning with their native English-speaking peers, who apprentice them into the language."

- Unlike her grade-level colleagues, Ms. Dennison doesn't use any small-group learning. Her instruction is strictly to the whole group. "That's the way I've always taught, and I'm not going to change now."

If you think this sounds like a study, you're right. Garrett and Hong (2016) analyzed the learning experiences of 3,748 kindergarten English learners, comparing these to the teacher's grouping practices and ratings of these students' math abilities. They found that teacher expectations and estimates of a student's achievement strongly influence a student's capacity to learn. This finding is in line with seminal studies on the Pygmalion effect (Rosenthal & Jacobson, 1968), showing that students' performance was influenced by their teachers' beliefs about them as learners, and Hattie's (2015) findings that teacher estimates of performance have an effect size of 1.62, equivalent to nearly three years' growth.

There is a lot we can learn from the outcome of Garrett and Hong's study of kindergartner English learners. You probably would not be surprised that students in classrooms like those of Ms. Dennison (whole-group instruction only) and Ms. Campbell (permanent homogenous grouping) received significantly lower teacher ratings of their ability. Importantly, these same classrooms spent more time on lower-level math instruction (below the average level of the class). Comparatively, the English learners in conditions similar to those found in Mr. Andrews's classroom (whole-group instruction with heterogeneous small groups) and Ms. Barnett's (whole-group instruction with a combination of homogenous and heterogeneous groups) received higher teacher estimates of their math skills, knowledge, and behaviors. And here's why that's important: *the students in these two conditions spent more time in high-level math instruction.* In other words, the students had more opportunities to learn than peers taught in whole-group or permanently homogenously grouped settings. The differences did not lie within the characteristics of the students, but in their exposure to challenging curriculum. It was the teachers' delivery of more or less rigorous curriculum and instruction that influenced their beliefs about students' abilities. Those teachers who spent more time teaching lower-level math skills and concepts, believed their students were less capable, while those who taught at higher levels believed their students to be more capable.

Why Opportunity to Learn Is Important for Equity

The opportunity to learn (or not) is a function of the systems we create in our classrooms and schools. Decades of research have demonstrated that the opportunity to learn is the major variable in student success. Few would disagree with the statement that a child's last name, skin color, or family income should never determine his or her future. But the systems and operational structures in schools and classrooms can do just that. When some students have access to challenging curriculum while others do not, inequity finds a breeding ground.

Inequitable Opportunities to Learn

Now imagine the multiplicative effect of these experiences and expectations played out across a student's academic career. Systematic exposure to less challenging curriculum results in depressed achievement—you simply can't learn what you haven't been taught. This concept, called the opportunity to learn (OTL), was first discussed by Carroll (1963) and has since been expanded by other researchers across several dimensions: instructional time, content or subject matter, and degree of complexity of skills and concepts. In elementary school, these are evidenced in terms of the relative amount of attention devoted to discrete skills versus critical thinking. Sadly, we have seen too many elementary classes where a group of students are consistently asked to read texts well below grade level and then are assigned worksheets that emphasize recall and recognition instead of critical thinking. It doesn't take long before these students become discouraged and develop negative beliefs about themselves and school in general. They come to distrust themselves as learners and habitually avoid tasks and situations that might highlight perceived shortcomings (Tschannen-Moran & Hoy, 2000). This distrust extends to "educational institutions, [which] inhibits learning... after years of failure, many students develop a wall of resistance that gets in the way of instruction" (Henson & Gilles, 2003, p. 260).

In secondary schools, this lack of opportunity to learn is further compounded by policies and procedures that promote a meritocracy in which students must earn their way into more challenging coursework. Those who fail to do so are relegated to remedial classes with less challenging coursework and are placed on a track to earn basic diplomas. Now think back to those kindergarten English learners we described in the opening scenario. By the time they get to middle school, the damage has been done. Their self-concepts as learners and their attitudes toward school are well established, and they are far less likely to advocate for a more challenging course of study. After all, they have learned less because they have been exposed to less than their same-age peers. In school systems that adhere to a meritocracy structure, where previous achievement determines future coursework, fewer students of color, students who have disabilities, students who are English learners, and students who are socioeconomically disadvantaged compared to peers are enrolled in advanced coursework.

We should pause to note that inequitable opportunities to learn are not confined to U.S. schools. In a study of the relationship between OTL, high school reading, and school systems, LaFontaine, Baye, Vieluf, and Monseur (2015) analyzed the 2009 Programme for International Student Assessment (PISA) data from 34 participant countries. As part of the assessment, students were asked how often in the previous month they had used literary and informational texts and what they did with them (i.e., retrieve information, analyze text, or reflect upon and critique text). The research team determined that the variance between schools, as measured by the reading achievement of these 15-year-olds, was greater in systems that offered tracked course-work (academic, technical, and vocational) than in those that did not. The OTL in these systems was primarily a function of socioeconomic status, and poorer students experienced a less-challenging curriculum. On the other hand, school systems that offered a more comprehensive structure, where classrooms were filled with students of mixed abilities, had a lower variance between schools. In these systems, the opportunity to learn from more challenging curriculum and instruction had somewhat less to do with socioeconomic status. Instead, these schools designed their systems such that a broader range of students participated in more challenging coursework. This statement from the Organisation for Economic Co-operation and Development (OECD) report is worthy enough to quote at length:

> Successful school systems—those that perform above average and show below-average socio-economic inequalities—provide all students, regardless of their socio-economic backgrounds, with similar opportunities to learn. Systems that show high performance and an equitable distribution of learning outcomes tend to be comprehensive, requiring teachers and schools to embrace diverse student populations through personalised educational pathways. In contrast, school systems that assume that students have different destinations with different expectations and differentiation in terms of how they are placed in schools, classes and grades often show less equitable outcomes without an overall performance advantage. (2010, p. 15)

The upshot is that achievement correlates with OTL. Not surprising, right? *It's hard to learn what you haven't been taught.* U.S. schools landed in the middle of the rankings of these 34 countries in the LaFontaine study, and we have the achievement to prove it: middling reading achievement results consistent with school policies that perpetuate the status quo. School and classroom systems are designed to obtain the results they get. In this chapter, we will address issues that affect a student's opportunity to learn from challenging curriculum. As with the other chapters, we'll conclude with a discussion of the associated guide statements on the Building Equity Review.

Modern-Day Segregation

The Atlantic magazine reported on an Office for Civil Rights finding against a New Jersey district with this attention-grabbing headline: "The Department of Education has branded 'tracking'—designating students for separate educational paths based on their academic performance—as a modern-day form of segregation" (Kohli, 2014). The inequalities and long-term inequities of previous decades of school segregation represent one of the United States' most debilitating and humiliating educational practices. Despite the fact that many of our schools remain racially segregated, at least we have evolved to the point that our laws do not prohibit integration. Instead, school segregation, as it exists today, is more a factor of ongoing economic disparities that affect neighborhood housing plans and demographics. But we further amplify these inequities when we perpetuate them in our schools under the guise of teaching.

Our institutional racism, or at least our institutional insensitivities, are now much less publicly apparent. As we look closer within each of our campuses, we are likely to find examples of practices that separate and segregate students. In fact, as the National Equity Project (NEP) has argued, students can be said to take *separate journeys through the same school* (U.S. Department of Education's Office for Civil Rights, 2016). The NEP has undertaken work to expose segregation-related inequities by calling for the examination of how school-based cultural attitudes, academic tracking, curricular access, and after-school activities serve as sorting mechanisms that set students on paths of success or failure. In the 1980s, the awareness that schools create different paths for students that predict their future success pushed educator and civil rights leader Bob Moses to begin the Baltimore Algebra Project (www.baltimorealgebraproject.org). Moses knew that algebra was a gatekeeper subject because it was necessary for advancing in other math and core subjects and for meeting college entrance requirements. He also knew that students of color were not being prepared for algebra and were in fact being systematically tracked out of algebra class. (This is an example of what we mean in the Building Equity Audit by school practices that thwart opportunity to learn.) In response, Moses formed the Baltimore Algebra Project as both an educational and civil rights initiative.

In its most obvious form, the separate paths students take become formal tracks based on ability or presumed ability. National attention and debate coalesced in 1985, when Jeannie Oakes wrote *Keeping Track: How Schools Structure Inequality.* Since that time, the negative effects of tracking have been well documented, and yet the U.S. Department of Education and Office for Civil Rights (2016) is still issuing citations to school districts for tracking students out of advanced and higher learning opportunities.

Separate and segregated tracks in our schools provide inequitable opportunities to learn. Some of our schools' class offerings, scheduling, and grouping strategies may not be as obvious as creating separate school tracks and will not garner the attention of the Office for Civil Rights. But these practices are still impeding opportunities for students to learn. We are not taking the position here that there is never occasion for using a wide range of grouping strategies. Rather, we are suggesting that the expectations we have and the assumptions we make about students' equal and equitable access to educational achievements must be examined. Both the Building Equity Review and the full Building Equity Audit are designed to provide evidence of practices that should, at the very least, be questioned.

Access to Challenging Curriculum

The academic intensity of a high school student's experience is a chief factor in determining his or her postsecondary options. It is also a primary factor in the decisions of college admissions officers. In a 2014 survey, 82 percent of National Association for College Admission Counseling members stated that grades in college-prep courses was of "considerable importance," followed by the strength of the curriculum (64 percent). This is in comparison to admission test scores (58 percent) and class rank (15 percent) (Clinedinst, 2015). But these figures reflect the relative status of students nearing the end of their K–12 academic careers. The road to completion of college- and career-ready curriculum begins upon entry into school. In this section, we will discuss how to set students on this path from the start. In keeping with backwards planning, we'll begin with the end in mind and then look at what it takes to get students there.

A pipeline from high school to postsecondary education

"My dad says that a high school diploma is your pants, and your undergraduate degree is your shirt," Qalaad, a recent graduate told us. "Your master's degree is your tie, and your PhD is your suit. No one's going to talk to you unless you at least have your pants and shirt on."

Qalaad is a first-generation immigrant from Somalia who came to the United States as a young child. Like so many other students at the school where we work, Qalaad has a family who has actively encouraged his educational attainment. But their encouragement is wasted unless the school their child attends intentionally structures itself so that he and all the other students can acquire the knowledge and skills needed for postsecondary education. And students like Qalaad are especially at risk because their parents, and most members of their communities, do not have personal experiences navigating the postsecondary landscape of the United States. They rely on us to build the pipeline their children need to move forward in their academic and professional careers.

Neither we nor the school where we work believes that the only path to success is a college degree. Postsecondary technical schools, military service, and immediate employment after graduation are worthy and valid options for any student. But we want to ensure that graduating students are as ably equipped as possible to make decisions about their future. That's why we do everything we can to get students involved in college admission testing. With newly expanded services, all students in 9th grade now take the PSAT, giving them a baseline measure of their readiness. Note that we also have 8th graders at our middle school take the PSAT, but some of our 9th graders have matriculated from other middle schools. We aggressively counsel (some say "bug") our students to take the SAT, and we use waivers to ensure that no one declines to take it due to financial hardships. We even provide buses to take them to the nearby school site where the Saturday SAT is administered, and on those days, we furnish both snacks and pencils. The principal and other administrators ride these buses too, showing up for moral support. Similarly, we support students who are interested in the military in studying and taking the Armed Services Vocational Aptitude Battery (ASVAB). The knowledge, skills, and dispositions our students develop through exposure to challenging curriculum position them to make the most of all these possibilities. What we *don't* want is for the young adults who learn with us to realize their options are limited because of particular courses they did or did not take when they were 14 years old.

It could be argued, and sometimes is, that because students arrive at high school with a broad range of academic knowledge, skills, and dispositions already in place, some students are not qualified for challenging course work. The results of a large-scale longitudinal study of students labeled as having a learning disability call this belief into question. Shifrer, Callahan, and Muller (2013) followed the academic trajectory of more than 16,000 high school students with learning disabilities from 10th grade through two years after school completion. The researchers compared these students' progress with that of peers who had similar academic, noncognitive, and behavioral histories but were not labeled as having a learning disability. The findings were striking. Only 4 percent of students identified as having a learning disability completed all the college preparatory courses available to them, compared with 38 percent of those with similar profiles but without the label. The researchers noted that while it is difficult to ascertain why this was so, they speculated that "the label shapes how adults perceive the student's ability and potential... and ultimately results in adults being less likely to guide the student toward challenging coursework" (p. 676). The questions for educators is, how many of our students could do challenging work if only we allowed and encouraged them to do so?

Perceptions and beliefs about students are powerful, and in many cases, they are reflections of subconcious biases rather than the result of intentional deliberation. Therefore, any equity audit should look at the percentage of students who complete challenging coursework. Many schools and districts are developing data systems to monitor placement in and completion of college preparatory coursework. Wise school leaders actively look for disparities among student subgroups and actively address these gaps. Innovative districts are removing barriers altogether by aligning basic high school graduation requirements with advanced diplomas. For example, in our state, California, to earn a college preparatory diploma, students must complete coursework that meets these "a–g requirements" (Regents of the University of California, 2015):

a: Two years of history/social sciences
b: Four years of college preparatory English
c: Three years of college preparatory Mathematics
d: Two years of laboratory science
e: Two years of the same language other than English
f: One year of visual and performing arts
g: One additional year of "elective" coursework selected from the a–f courses

Ours is a health sciences school, so we felt that it was essential for our students to not only meet a–g requirements but to also have four years of science and mathematics. This has become our default diploma pathway. Rather than expecting young adolescents and their families to anticipate and then advocate for a college preparatory course of study, we enroll all of them (including students with significant disabilities) in these classes beginning in 9th grade. To be sure, some students need substantially more support to be successful in these demanding courses. After all, simply plunking a kid into a challenging course and then keeping your fingers crossed is nothing more than wishful thinking. *Hope*, as they say, *is not a plan*, which is why our school has also developed a system of compensatory and adaptive interventions, which will be detailed later in this chapter.

An academic emphasis in middle school

"My plan to make my dream come true is to push myself academically and not slack off when I'm in, like, math class or any other classes." So said Reuben, a 7th grader being interviewed by Staci Benak, one of the talented math teachers we work with. Staci's middle school curriculum emphasizes the role of engineering and design, and Reuben has said that he wants to become an engineer for the military. We hope he achieves this dream, and we are committed to getting him there. But for the moment, let's not focus on his aspiration, which will be years in the making. What Staci asks Reuben and every student she works with to do is discuss their plans for making their dreams a reality. Fostering the aspirations of the adolescents we teach is insufficient, and downright cruel, if we don't also help them see how their actions today are a ladder to tomorrow. It does us no good to have students claim that they want to be teachers (and yet hate to read), veterinarians (but fail science), or military engineers (but slack off in math class). Middle school is a time when we must foster students' understanding of how the quality of their middle school experience sets the stage for high school.

Let's talk a little more about the PSAT. This test, administered to 8th graders, provides a great opportunity to talk with students about their current actions and dispositions and where those might be strengthened. We discuss their attendance data with them and share findings about the effects of chronic absenteeism, defined as missing 18 or more school days in a year. Many of our students are shocked to learn that even one year of chronic absenteeism in secondary school increases a student's likelihood of dropping out sevenfold (U.S. Department of Education, 2016). Because we know that certain subgroups are more vulnerable, we monitor attendance and make home visits to involve families. For example, because we're aware that students with disabilities are 34 percent more likely to be absent than peers without disabilities (U.S. Department of Education, 2016), a discussion about attendance is part of every IEP meeting.

Other key components in our approach are sharing data with students and working with them to create student-directed learning goals. The power of these kinds of goals is well documented; Hattie (2015) reports that they have an effect size of 1.44, which is equivalent to more than three years' worth of growth in a single school year. Goal setting is also developmentally appropriate for young adolescents, who are trying on new identities (sometimes bewilderingly so) and exercising their autonomy (sometimes puzzlingly so). Therefore, students learn about themselves academically in the first weeks of school. One example comes from a reading diagnostic test that provides the student with a quantitative reading level. Many schools do similar assessments, but it's important to take the extra step of sharing these results with students and transforming them into goals. The results are coupled with lessons on the reading expectations for each grade level, and students are guided by the teacher to set quarterly goals for advancement. Each student completes an online reading assessment every week or two, then confers with the teacher on progress toward stated goals. To be clear, the magic is not in the assessment—it's in the follow-up from a caring adult who discusses the results and helps the student to plan next steps. These conversations allow the student and teacher to discuss academic and noncognitive behaviors (e.g., persistence, help-seeking, organization, self-regulation) that may be aiding or impeding progress. At a time when young adolescents are experimenting with their autonomy, we want them to understand just how powerfully they can positively direct their own lives.

Stage setting in the elementary grades

"I love school! I love art and I love the library and I love the bean plants we're growing and I even love lunch!" So said 1st grader Bella. Well, maybe "said" isn't the right term, as she made this claim in a singsong voice and accessorized it with a bit of the twirling around that 6-year-olds are known for. Bella's love of school is what we hope all our children will experience during their elementary years. Yet Bella's life is beset with challenges. Her family is undocumented, having escaped the violence of a Central American nation that had already claimed the lives of an older sister and her paternal grandparents. Because her mom and dad don't speak much English and work multiple jobs, it is difficult for them to actively participate at her school. Fortunately for Bella, her elementary school is structured to support her success. The school offers a number of community-based programs, such as hosting parent meetings in local churches to increase the comfort and confidence of families. In addition, the school works closely with other agencies to help families obtain health and dental services.

But the real strides this school has made in the past few years are attributable to the elimination of in-grade retention policies, the careful structuring of heterogeneous classes, and an investment in innovative cross-curricular approaches. Each of these policies and practices has enhanced the opportunities to learn for Bella and her peers. The first significant change was the elimination of a longstanding mandatory retention policy in 1st and 3rd grades. In-grade retention seems to have a lock on the imagination of so many educators, who sincerely believe that an extra year at the same grade level will give young children the time they need to "catch up." However, the overwhelming evidence does not bear out this belief:

- Any short-term academic benefits disappear within three years of retention. Retention in kindergarten is especially harmful for future mathematics achievement (Vandecandelaere, Vansteelandt, De Fraine, & Van Damme, 2016).
- Early-grade retention is among the strongest predictors of dropping out in high school (Jimerson, Anderson, & Whipple, 2002).
- Elementary students retained because of low reading achievement did not make gains and were consistently outperformed through 8th grade by similarly achieving students who were not retained (Silberglitt, Appleton, Burns, & Jimerson, 2006).
- Retention was found to be the only school-based practice that had a negative effect size (d = -0.17) (Hattie, 2015).

We'll cite one last heartbreaking study on the issue of retention. Young schoolchildren reported that the only thing they feared more than "being held back" was the death of a parent, and they reported that they would rather "wet in class" than face a second year in the same grade (Byrnes & Yamamoto, 1985).

In the face of decades of overwhelming evidence that in-grade retention policies do not yield academic gains, and are corrosive to the self-concepts of children to the extent that they shorten academic careers, Bella's district reversed its policy on mandatory retention. They coupled these efforts with extensive professional learning for teachers and administrators about alternatives to in-grade retention. Now, any time a teacher wants to recommend retention, he or she must meet with a school-site panel to produce evidence of what interventions have taken place. "Our Student Study Team has been instrumental in changing the conversation," said Linda Walters, the principal of Bella's school. "When a child is showing signs of being at academic risk, we need to move swiftly to intervene. But simply doing more of the same and expecting a different result just doesn't make any sense." And no longer do these questions and responses wait until the end of the year. There is no delay in suggesting, providing, evaluating, and adjusting interventions for students who are showing signs of being at academic risk.

A second change process at Bella's school has focused on building classes more thoughtfully. Past practice had been somewhat laissez faire. Kindergartners filled class rosters in order of enrollment. Once one class was filled, a new one began, resulting in very uneven distributions in terms of gender, language proficiency, and need for specialized supports. Bella's school now uses the kindergarten readiness data they collect during individual orientation sessions with parents, either at their preschool or during a family visit, to build stronger classes. They employ an alternate ranking system based on these variables as well as skills, assigning students to one of four groups, each containing 25 percent of the students. Within each group, students are rank ordered:

1. High academic skills, high social-emotional skills
2. High academic skills, developing social-emotional skills
3. Developing academic skills, developing social-emotional skills
4. Developing academic skills, high social-emotional skills

Preliminary rosters are then generated by pairing students in groups 1 and 3 together in equal numbers, while other classes are composed of students drawn equally from groups 2 and 4. This allows for heterogeneous grouping, but with range limitations that don't make the span too broad within any one classroom. The preliminary rosters are then examined by a team composed of the principal, grade-level chair, social worker, counselor, special education teacher, and English learner coordinator. They make changes as needed to balance gender and specialized support needs. After discussing the characteristics of each class, the team makes recommendations to the principal regarding teacher assignments. These rosters are updated during the summer as students enroll, and teacher assignments are announced just before the school year begins.

"I'm especially cautious about teachers who are new to the school or new to the profession," said Ms. Walters. "I want to make sure I'm setting them up for success." When enrollment after the beginning of the school year requires that a new class be added, it's Ms. Walters who rebuilds the class rosters. She recalled being a young teacher who was hired after the start of the school year, and her first class assignment was composed of all of the students the existing teachers wanted out of their rooms. "It was a nightmare. I was the least experienced on the team, and got a class of the hardest-to-teach students." Vowing that she would never do the same to new teachers, she takes care to reconstitute classes more equitably. "Seriously, we eat our young. If we want to deliver a world-class education, then we need to pay attention to how we can best make our teachers successful, too."

The third prong of this school's efforts to increase the opportunity to learn by giving all students access to challenging curriculum is through its commitment to a STEAM (science, technology, engineering, arts, and math) program. While the long-term effectiveness of STEAM is still unknown, the true potential of it may be in the ways it prompts elementary teachers to reconsider how these disciplines are linked, and how students can apply creativity and critical thinking skills to resolve problems. Since moving in this direction, Ms. Walters has witnessed a new level of teacher collaboration, one born out of new purposes. "Rather than grade-level teams doling out traditional assignments, they are finding some renewed vigor in considering design, engineering, and arts as essential components of their science and math instruction," she said. Teacher collaboration is an important driver in student achievement. A large-scale study of 47 elementary schools compared levels of teacher collaboration to mathematics and reading achievement of more than 2,500 4th graders, finding a significant positive correlation between the two (Goddard, Goddard, & Tschannen-Moran, 2007). The researchers reached this conclusion:

> Based on the results of this study, we believe that if teachers in urban elementary schools have the potential to raise student achievement on high-stakes mathematics and reading assessments through collaboration, such efforts should be encouraged and supported. (p. 892)

Ms. Walters concurred. "We knew that offering all students increased access to challenging curriculum required increasing teacher collaboration. It's my responsibility to put structures into place that allow for meaningful teacher collaboration. If we're committed to increasing opportunities to learn for all the children at this school, then maintaining these structures, and keeping an eye out for erosion of these structures, is critical."

Human and Social Capital

Much has been written about the need to increase the skill and knowledge levels of young people to prepare them for secure futures. These skills are often referred to collectively as *21st century skills*, a term we find ironic given that we are almost 20 percent into that century. However they are named, they are of great value. Many 21st century skills fall into the realm of *soft skills*, including communication, collaboration, creativity, and critical thinking. Others are categorized as *life and career skills*, such as self-direction, flexibility, leadership, and responsibility (P21 Partnership for 21st Century Learning, 2015). But one element that can be overlooked in curriculum audits is whether students have opportunities to amass human capital, the "broad set of cognitive skills and knowledge that is necessary today, along with interpersonal skills such as collaboration and teamwork" (Kirsch, Braun, Lennon, & Sands, 2016, p. 3).

Social capital is a related construct. It's a truism of life is that "it's not what you know, it's *who* you know." Some students and, in fact, some readers of this book must acknowledge that the good fortune they have enjoyed in their lives is due to whom they have known, and perhaps more important, who has known them. Social capital describes the network of relationships one has through family, friends, community, and school or work. Access to human and social capital begins before birth and is affected by access to health care and nutrition, the parents' level of education, and income. While schools have a less direct influence on some of these elements, other gates are entirely erected by schools. These include entry and screening requirements that place young children in remedial groups, tracked courses in secondary schools, and suspension and expulsion practices that result in a disproportionate number of students of color, students with disabilities, and students with language differences being excluded from instruction (U.S. Department of Education Office for Civil Rights, 2014).

Increasing OTL requires that students are present and in attendance. They need to be at school in order to take advantage of the human and social capital that is built through meaningful contact with peers and educators who can create new possibilities. Exclusionary policies that thwart enrollment in challenging courses mean that some students must confront another gate that stymies their progress. Even if they gain enrollment, discipline policies can also systematically exclude them from class, resulting in less time in rigorous instructional settings. And when you're not there at all, or even some of the time, your human and social capital is compromised. Opportunities to learn soft skills, life skills, and career skills are missed. Not there because you were suspended on the day the guest speaker came to discuss women in science research? A missed opportunity. Not enrolled in an advanced mathematics because no one counseled you about its importance? That means the instructor never got to know you, so she didn't mention you to a college recruiter looking for talented students of color. You spend significant amounts of time in the company of other struggling readers? That means you didn't read the Sandra Cisneros short stories enjoyed by the rest of the class, so you never discovered that another classmate found his voice through writing, just like you could have. These missed opportunities, although impossible to measure quantitatively, pile up. The accumulated result is diminished human and social capital to draw upon. Although we often examine the relative resiliency of children, we rarely analyze the amount of human and social capital they have. Simply stated, if students' opportunities to learn are limited, so too will be the human and social capital they are likely to accumulate.

Elk Lake School District took on the issue of human and social capital in a comprehensive way. After conducting an audit of their district processes, they identified a number of gates that served as obstacles for their most vulnerable children and families, including

- A kindergarten screening process that was used to place students in homogeneous classrooms.
- A lack of translation services at elementary information nights, which resulted in families who did not speak English failing to enroll their children in summer school services and enrichment activities.
- A tracked system of courses in middle and high school that included honors and remedial sections.
- A failure to monitor the number of 9th grade students enrolled in Algebra 1, meaning that those who did not enroll as 9th graders could not complete an advanced mathematical sequence of study.
- A failure to provide information about college financial, scholarship, and application procedures to high school families until students reached 11th grade, which was far too late for those who didn't already anticipate or have experience with these complicated processes.

The district sought to rectify these policy issues to increase opportunities to learn, with an eye toward developing human and social capital. Not surprisingly, they began at the high school level, first eliminating tracked courses and instituting a new policy called Honors for All. "Every student, any student, can earn honors credit for a course without consequences," explained curriculum director Antonio Guerrero. Now all 9th grade students are enrolled in Algebra 1, and additional tutoring time is provided for those who need support. In addition, Elk Grove reconfigured college and career outreach to families by scheduling meetings and conferences and setting up information booths at community events. "We've had an outstanding response, as families are learning about postsecondary options much sooner," explained Mr. Guerrero. "Now we're getting to talk to families with children in middle school."

Sara Hernandez, the district's elementary curriculum director, added that in addition to far more robust translation and outreach services for elementary family members, the major change was the class construction. "Through the audit process we came face to face with the inequities of our long-held class placement practices, which involved the teacher rating each child on a scale of 1 to 5 for behavior, academics, and relationships with peers. Then the teachers would barter. 'I'll take this kid, but then you have to take these two.' We responded by providing extensive professional trainings with principals and grade-level chairs on how to build class rosters more equitably." Ms. Hernandez and Mr. Guerrero acknowledged that there is still work to be done. "What's that saying, that the last thing a fish notices is the water it swims in? We're taking steps to notice our water quality, and then to address it."

Building Equity Review Statements: Opportunity to Learn

The opportunity to learn expectation requires that individuals within schools consider the ways in which students are scheduled and placed into classes. It also requires that teachers believe that students can learn and that challenging learning experiences are provided. Now, let's focus on the six guiding statements in the Opportunity to Learn level of the Building Equity Review and examine efforts schools have taken in response to adapt equity-promoting policies and practices.

11. *We do not use tracking to group or schedule students.*

This tracking statement serves as the beacon for the other statements that follow. This is the first item in the Level 3 section, and many of the items that follow this guiding statement assume an affirmative response and prompt a closer look at practices used to decide on schedules, offerings, and groupings.

We know that measures and presumptions of student ability are often based on previous inequities in opportunities to learn; continuing to track students exacerbates those existing inequities.

Earlier in this chapter, we described Bob Moses's work with the Baltimore Algebra Project as having educational and civil rights implications. Moses knew that the postsecondary fate of graduates was being predetermined by decisions about whether to offer high school algebra to certain students—and that this was disproportionately affecting students of color negatively. The simple response would be to just place all 9th graders in Algebra 1; then, of course, critics would object, arguing that this amounts to placing students who are math deficient and lack prerequisite skills in classes in which they are destined to fail. You've probably heard the argument: *putting all 9th graders in Algebra 1, regardless of their readiness is not fair to the students, to their teachers, to or to the other students who* are *ready for this level of math. Some 9th graders need a pre-algebra class.* Dr. Lou Brown, our longtime friend and colleague from the University of Wisconsin, and an advocate for full inclusion of people with disabilities into school and the community, faced this logic throughout his career. He had a simple and factually substantiated response at the ready: "*Pre* means never." And, as we noted earlier in this chapter, students are not going to learn what they are never taught.

At the same time, we know from experience that placing students who have a history of struggling in math in algebra may be equal treatment, but the placement alone does not constitute equitable practice. We made the argument that inequities need to be challenged by improvements throughout the preK–12 system. So how do we respond to the 9th grade Alison, who is about to walk into the algebra classroom having experienced 10 years of educational inequities? If we do not ask that question, we are likely to contribute to Alison's failure rather than her success. Bob Moses was aware of this reality. The Baltimore Algebra Project was not just about access, it was about equity. In order to overcome previous inequities, we have to do the heavy lifting required to support a student's forward progress. Treading water gets them nowhere.

Clearly, any school undertaking the bold and necessary steps to open up opportunities to learn for all students must be prepared to allocate new resources or reallocate existing resources. Response to Intervention (RTI) is an excellent example of reallocation of resources. So is the movement from self-contained and remedial classes (such as a special day class or special education world history) to inclusive models. These practices allow a school to reallocate resources so that push-in staff, smaller class sizes, co-teaching arrangements, and curricular modification and adaptations can help a broader spectrum of students.

12. *Students have equitable access to class placement and course offerings.*

As we have noted, it's critical to get students into integrated school settings and to support their social and emotional engagement. But that's just a start. We also have to ensure that they get into classes and courses equitably rather than based on a demographic variable.

Brenda Jesperson is quite skilled in supporting the needs of students with behavioral challenges. Her classroom routines and procedures are clear, and she has a sophisticated understanding of restorative practices that allow students to learn from the harm that they cause others. As a result of this unique skill set in her school, Ms. Jesperson started to get all of the students who had been identified as "behaviorally challenging."

With all of the "challenging" kids going to Ms. Jesperson year after year, none of the other teachers on her grade-level team needed to get any better at meeting behavioral learning needs. Over time, Ms. Jesperson started spending more and more of her time teaching students prosocial behaviors. At some point, she realized that she was no longer as effective in academic support, and she began worrying that her students, both those with and without behavioral challenges, would suffer academically. This is a fairly typical example of an inequitable placement practice—unfair to Ms. Jesperson, unfair to her colleagues, and unfair to her students.

It wasn't too long ago that female students were routinely counseled out of enrolling in challenging science classes. Doug's mom tells the story of how her high school counselor explained that she did not need chemistry because she'd be better served by working on her "Mrs." degree than by trying to go to college. Largely because she had followed the scheduling advice of her counselor, she graduated from high school without having completed the required courses for college admission.

Students should not be placed in classes or courses of study based on their demographics or the expectations of those with the power to assign students to their schedule. Instead, there should be a transparent way that classes are built in the master schedule so that every student has a chance to enroll in challenging learning environments. Of course there are logical prerequisite conditions that must be taken into account in some high school classes. Having said that, people devoted to equity will analyze class placements to determine if there was any bias in the formation of groups.

This is exactly what the teachers at Bell Elementary School did. They used to have a "card party," as they called it. Every student had a card, and on that card were stickers to indicate various demographic characteristics and support needs, ranging from skin color to languages spoken to special needs to giftedness. During the card party, teachers would trade cards to form their ideal group of students and "pass" on those they would rather not teach. You might have heard "deals" like this pitched: "I'll give you two gifted students if you take this English learner. I just don't think that he would do well in my class."

Unfortunately, targeted placements of students are not limited to elementary school. In fact, the problem gets worse as students get older. We haven't ever seen a card party in a high school, but we do know that teachers tell the counselors which students they believe would do best in their classes. Several years ago, we overheard an English teacher tell the counselor, "Don't put any disabled students in my class. I teach honors, and they don't belong in there." An analysis of the master schedule reveals a wide range of biases that adults within the school have. Addressing those biases is important if equity efforts are going to thrive. Again, we're not simply suggesting that students be placed in classes at random or that they won't need additional supports to be successful. We are saying that equity efforts that fail to address placement within classes are doomed to failure.

13. *All students have access to challenging curriculum.*

We have argued elsewhere (e.g., Fisher, Frey, & Hattie, 2016) that there is a difference between difficulty and complexity. To our thinking, difficult curriculum requires more time, effort, and work, whereas complex curriculum involves multiple steps, application of significant background knowledge, and strategic thinking. For there to be sufficient challenge, both difficulty and complexity need to be present. If tasks are just difficult, meaning that they simply take a lot of time and effort rather than call on involved thinking, students will become frustrated and angry with school. If there is insufficient challenge, a range of negative consequences begin to pile up, including the following chain reaction:

1. Students become bored and less motivated to engage in school. *As a result…*
2. Students do not complete assigned tasks. *Consequently…*
3. Students are not prepared for future challenges. *Thus, they seem unprepared and…*
4. Future decisions about access to rigorous curriculum are derailed because there is a perception that students are not ready. *And the result is…*
5. Students do not have access to equitable outcomes.

Breaking this chain starts by ensuring access to complex, relevant, and interesting classes and classwork. The challenging part is the how.

The way forward depends a lot on the individual school's circumstances. The teachers at Parkview Elementary School are provided time to observe other teachers as part of the walkthrough system they have developed. Groups of teachers identify problems of practice and then visit classrooms to figure out if their peers have solved this problem. Parkview teachers had been engaged in this process for several years, and were comfortable with visitors and this inquiry cycle, when one of the groups wanted to know how teachers helped students master grade-level concepts. They went to observe several classrooms and noted that in every case, the task expectations were not on grade level, even though the standards identified were on grade level.

This led to a very interesting conversation. As one of the teachers noted, "We think we are teaching students at high levels, but the curriculum that we actually use is not at the same level of expectation. No wonder our students struggle when they get to middle school. They aren't as prepared as we thought they were."

Another said, "After our last walkthroughs, I went to look at my curriculum and the tasks that are assigned. I don't think that they were very rigorous. I think we need to add some rigor to our curriculum and then figure out what we need to do to make sure that students can master the curriculum."

This, then, became their problem of practice. As a group, they began to develop different tasks from those assigned in the textbook that they had been using for several years. For example, during a reading of the poem "Paul Revere's Ride" by Henry Wadsworth Longfellow, students were asked to respond to the following prompt: *Think about what it might have been like to be a patriot in Massachusetts at the time of Revere's ride. What do you think it may have been like to make that ride?*

"It's pretty low level to have students think about what it would have been like to ride at that time," one teacher pointed out. "I mean, they can really say just about anything that they want, and they don't even have to use the text in their answer."

As a group, they revised some of the discussion questions to ensure that students would be challenged. The new ones read like this:

- Do you think that being alone while riding on his difficult path makes Paul Revere more or less heroic? Explain your opinion.
- The poet uses a rhyme structure. What effect do you think the rhyming words might have on a reader?
- What does the speaker mean by "the fate of a nation was riding that night"?

Notice how each of these questions requires a deeper understanding of the poem's meaning.

The team also updated the writing prompt to read as follows: *What kind of person do you think Paul Revere was? What evidence in the poem can you cite to support these characteristics?* Now, students had to form an opinion and then explain that opinion with evidence from the text. As a team, they agreed that the lesson was much more challenging than it had been previously. As one of the teachers noted, "I really thought that my lessons were directly aligned with the standards, so I would be frustrated that the state assessment scores weren't as good as I expected. It wasn't the test, it was the curriculum that we were using. It has to be challenging for students to master the skills they need."

Sometimes, well-meaning educators take a developmental approach to students' learning rather than ensuring that all students have access to challenging course content. In these cases, teachers identify students' current level of performance and teach them at that level, hoping that they will make sufficient progress. As one teacher told us, "I meet my students where they are. They are all individuals and my job is to help them grow. As long as they grow, I'm happy. I don't believe that they all need to get to the same place."

This is problematic from an equity standpoint. Yes, every student is an individual. And yes, our collective role is to ensure that all students grow. But meeting students where they are and then not ensuring that they have access to challenging learning experiences that accelerate the speed of their learning will likely result in deeper gaps in performance. Access is an important aspect of equity, and access to challenging learning experiences starts students on the road toward success.

This was the case when the teachers at Vista Point High School decided to eliminate low-level math classes and instead enroll all students in a rigorous course of study. Previously, students took an assessment during the first week of school and then were placed in a leveled math class based on their scores. The result was that some students had access to a rigorous curriculum, but others did not. A major motivator for the change came from a few honest students who said that they intentionally scored lower on the pre-assessment so that they could get easier math classes. As one of them said, "My transcript still says Geometry, but I took a slower version of it with students who were less prepared. I got an *A* because it was pretty easy for me. But if I'm honest, I feel a little guilty because I cheated the system."

To our thinking, it wasn't just the system that was cheated but also the student himself. He had access to a less rigorous curriculum that placed him at risk for learning less and, subsequently, for having less access to future learning. Eventually, this caught up to him. He did not perform well on the college math entrance exam and had to take several remedial math classes in college.

The change to a more inclusive sequence of math courses was initiated by teachers at Vista Point. They were not forced to change but rather proposed changes because of their discussion of the statement *"All students have access to challenging curriculum."* They understood that this new sequence would require a "heavy lift," as one of them said. So they set about scheduling additional tutorials for students and meeting with parents to talk about the need for all students to master mathematics to be successful in college. They also hired a retired teacher to push into classrooms and meet with small groups of students while the rest of the class engaged in collaborative problem solving. The results of Vista Point's efforts were impressive. Their mathematics achievement scores doubled the first year of implementation, and more students than ever took advanced mathematics in their senior year. In fact, for the first time, 60 percent of the Vista Point senior class was eligible for entrance into college mathematics without even taking the entrance exam. As one of the teachers commented, "I think we've changed the mindset of students. They know that they're in a challenging course of study and that there are supports for them to be successful. Focusing on access to challenging curriculum changed the experiences our students had."

14. *Teachers have high expectations for all students.*

There is a complex interaction between expectations and achievement, partly influenced by what adults are willing to see and partly influenced by the opportunities they provide, based on what they expect. We want the expectations we set to be high, and yet they also must be attainable. Doug's running coach saying that a marathon is a goal within reach is different from saying that Doug will win the Olympic marathon. Students need to believe the expectations they face are achievable.

Expectations also have to be communicated. When expectations are clear, and feedback is provided about efforts to achieve the expectation, students begin to take ownership and assume responsibility. We cannot tell you how many times we have said to a student, "Right now, I want this for you more than you want it for yourself. If we are going to be successful, you have to want it at least as much as I want it." These words aren't an abdication of our responsibility but an invitation to students to broaden their expectations for themselves and what they can achieve.

Take Abdi for example. He identified as an average student. During a meeting with him, the counselor suggested that he enroll in a college political science class being offered during the summer on his high school campus. As the counselor said, "You indicated that you wanted to go to college. Why not start now? It's a college class, but we will have support available to help you study and do well. Also, this class will meet your government graduation requirement, so you won't have to take that class during your senior year."

Abdi agreed to take the class, and his parents gladly signed the enrollment paperwork. It was a six-week class, designed to move fast—faster than anything Abdi had experienced before. During the first session, the support staff member assigned to the class noted that Abdi wasn't taking notes and had not completed the introductory letter the professor had requested. Afterward, in a meeting with Abdi, the support staff member said, "I expect that you will get an *A* in this class. To do so, you need to take notes and review those notes. I'm here to help you study during the lab time, but you'll need the notes to use your time well."

On Day 2 of the class, Abdi starting taking notes. Class that day ended with a pop quiz about the readings and the lecture. Abdi earned a *B*. During his next meeting with a support staff member, there was another conversation.

"I still expect that you'll get an *A* in this class, Abdi," the support staff member said. "That was just a quiz, remember. There's a test on Friday. What do you think you need to do to really know this stuff?" Abdi answered that he needed to read the chapter during lab and then talk with classmates about the reading. The staff member said, "I agree that a study group would be a good choice. I think that will help you earn your *A* in this class."

These meetings continued almost daily for the first two weeks of the course. Over that period of time, Abdi assumed increased responsibility for his own learning and, through his study group work, for the learning of others in the class. He ended up with an *A*. Afterward, Abdi admitted, "I was intimidated at first, thinking that I wasn't good enough for college. But everyone thought I could do it, so I decided that they weren't lying to me. I stepped up my game and did it. Now I want it myself. I know I can do it." Abdi took several additional college classes during his senior year and graduated high school with 15 units of college credits completed.

Of course, when teachers have and communicate low expectations for their students, students are likely to meet those expectations as well. Mary Castle used to say about her 4th graders, "They can't learn to write like this." She was referring to the anchor papers that were published by her state department of education and designed to help teachers score student writing. The wall of her classroom devoted to student writing had samples from the state and an occasional piece of student work. When asked about this wall, Ms. Castle said, "My students don't write very well, so I don't want them to see examples of bad writing. I only want them to see *good* writing, so I only put up student work when it is really good." Ms. Castle did not believe in her students, much less her ability to influence her students' learning. This became a self-fulfilling prophecy; each year her students' writing was judged inferior by external reviewers, both at the district and state levels.

There's a twist to this story. By the time these same students were given the state writing assessment in 7th grade, most of them scored at the proficient or advanced levels. What happened in that three-year window to change their performance so dramatically? Pablo De Rossa happened.

Mr. De Rossa was the "lead learner" (as he describes himself) for the English department at the middle school that most of Ms. Castle's students went on to attend. He was passionate about writing and believed that every student "had a story worth telling someplace inside them." His enthusiasm for students' writing was infectious, and he and his fellow English teachers spent significant amounts of time analyzing students' writing to determine what students still needed to be taught. They designed and delivered excellent lessons to close the gaps between students' current performance and teachers' expectations. These expectations were high, and they were communicated to students on a daily basis. Students were able to see their writing scores improve over the course of their 6th grade year, and they started to believe what their teachers kept telling them, namely that they could effectively express themselves in writing.

A chance meeting between Ms. Castle and Mr. De Rossa at a district conference changed Ms. Castle's world forever. Mr. De Rossa told Ms. Castle about a student they shared, Karla. Mr. De Rossa talked about Karla's writing and how she was able to describe situations so vividly. He went on to say that she scored proficient on her 7th grade assessment and was currently working on her graduation speech. Ms. Castle was dumbfounded, and the look on her face gave it away. "You look shocked!" Mr. De Rossa said. "Was Karla not as good a writer when she was with you?"

Ms. Castle shook her head in wonder. "You just named the worst writer in my class," she said, "and you're telling me about how much she has grown. I would have never predicted that. In fact, I would have guessed that Karla would fail English and even need to be retained."

Their conversation continued for several minutes. To her credit, Ms. Castle expressed both sincere admiration and considerable curiosity about Mr. De Rossa's approach. "I think I'd better come take a look at what you all are doing," she said. "I know that kids grow up a lot in middle school, but if the kids I had are writing that well now, maybe I need to make some changes in what I'm doing."

The probable truth was that Ms. Castle needed to make changes in curriculum and instruction so that her students could learn to write. But it was equally important for her to believe they were capable of being great writers. She had to be clear on her expectations for all of her students and communicate those expectations to them while also providing the support each of them needed to succeed. That's equitable practice.

15. *There are active working relationships between home and school to increase opportunities to learn.*

Opportunities to learn are not limited to the school day, and teachers are not the only ones who provide learning opportunities, much less make placement decisions or advocate for students. Parents and other family members are important allies in efforts to ensure equitable experiences and outcomes for all students. That's not to say that all parents are equally informed, which is where we will start with the discussion about relationships with family members.

First, our horror story. We were in a parent meeting, talking about the problematic behavior of a 9th grader we'll call Anisa. All of her teachers were in the room, and each had a chance to list the transgressions Anisa had committed. At one point, a teacher said that Anisa was just getting up and walking out of class in the middle of the period. The student's mom responded, "I'll send her tomorrow in diapers, and then she'll have no reason to leave the room." We weren't sure that this parent was taking the discussion seriously, and we continued to share some of the more egregious complaints. Then, with what sounded like complete seriousness, the mom said, "If she does that again, I'll kill her cat, and she will learn."

"Please," we said, "don't kill the cat. And don't send her in diapers." We vowed never to call this parent with a complaint again. It was an understandable reaction, but when we reflected on it, we agreed it was the wrong one. What we needed to do was build a bond with this student and this parent so that we could guide the experiences Anisa had at school and at home. We took stock of where things stood. Anisa had experienced poor instruction in her past, had been retained, and had been tracked into remedial classes. She and her family had come to believe that she was a failure. Our work with Anisa wasn't easy, and it took a lot of time and ongoing conversations with her and with her mom. By the time she graduated, Anisa had passed her classes (rigorous ones, we might add) and was admitted into a nursing assistant program. Her mom did not kill the cat and learned a lot about parenting. One of the things *we* learned was that Anisa's mom had obtained custody of her daughter only a few years before we met them; at the time, she was doing the best that she knew how to do.

Thankfully, most parents want to support the school and are willing to lend a hand when asked. Not every parent wants to volunteer in the class and, in fact, many feel uncomfortable in the educator role, but there any number of ways that parents can be involved. Epstein and her colleagues (2002) identified several categories of outreach schools might explore:

- **Parenting.** Assist families with parenting skills, family support, understanding child and adolescent development, and setting home conditions to support learning at each age and grade level. Assist schools in understanding families' backgrounds, cultures, and goals for children.
- **Communicating.** Communicate with families about school programs and student progress. Create two-way communication channels between school and home.
- **Volunteering.** Improve recruitment, training, activities, and schedules to involve families as volunteers and as audiences at the school or in other locations. Enable educators to work with volunteers who support students and the school.
- **Learning at home.** Involve families with their children in academic learning at home, including homework, goal setting, and other curriculum-related activities. Encourage teachers to design homework that enables students to share and discuss interesting tasks at home.
- **Decision making.** Include families as participants in school decisions, governance, and advocacy activities through school councils or improvement teams, committees, and parent organizations.
- **Collaborating with the community.** Coordinate resources and services for families, students, and the school with community groups, including businesses, agencies, cultural and civic organizations, and colleges or universities. Enable members of each of these community groups to contribute to the overall well-being of the family and school.

The approaches listed communicate to family members that they are valued. Having said that, equity efforts rely on parents being informed about the decisions that are being made about their children, especially when it comes to school and classroom placement.

Parents should be seen as partners in the process of education; no parent should find out after the fact that his or her child needed additional help and could have gotten it. That is what happened to Christopher's parents, who were told at the end of the school year that their son should be retained in kindergarten. According to his teacher, Christopher "wasn't academically ready for 1st grade" and instead should repeat kindergarten. Concerned for their son, Christopher's parents asked what they could do to help him improve. In response, the kindergarten teacher gave the family a packet of work that was well over 100 pages long. She said to them, "If Christopher can do this over the summer, then we can talk about moving him on to 1st grade. If not, he'll stay in kindergarten with me."

The packet of work was difficult. There was page after page of unrelated tasks for Christopher to do. Thinking that they were being helpful, Christopher's parents made him work on the packet regularly over the summer and did not do any of the work for him. Christopher regularly told his parents that he was "stupid" and "dumb" and that he "hated school." Yes, a 5-year-old was already thinking this about himself. The end of the summer came, and Christopher had not mastered the concepts in the packet. So he was assigned to the same kindergarten classroom, led by the same teacher. Within two weeks, Christopher was begging not to go to school. He was misbehaving in the class and was sent to the principal's office regularly. He cried when his parents dropped him off in the morning.

Now we should let you know that Christopher is black—one of the few black students attending a school with high enrollments of Latino/Hispanic and Pacific Islander students. With Christopher's status as an outsider clearer, you'll probably start wondering the same things we did. Could it be that he had to perform better than others to be considered for promotion? Was his teacher conflating behavior with academic achievement? What didn't Christopher's teacher communicate early and regularly with his parents—as soon as she started seeing signs that he was not meeting expectations?

Back to the story. Troubled by how miserable their son had become, Christopher's parents applied for a transfer and went on to enroll him in a choice program school in a historic part of the city. They told the front office staff that Christopher had been retained and was still in kindergarten. A reading specialist, Jodie Clarke, met with Christopher while his family was present. She interviewed him and praised his responses. Then Ms. Clarke told Christopher that she had a favorite book, and it was the third one in the pile on her desk. Could he go pick it up, so that she could share it with his parents? Christopher followed directions perfectly and retrieved the book. Next, Ms. Clarke asked if he would like to read the book with her, because there were two different voices in the book. Christopher did so, with few errors. Then Ms. Clarke asked if he would like to finish reading the book, because she needed to talk with his parents. While he did so, she turned his parents. "Christopher should be in 1st grade," she said, "and with your support, he will succeed. I just know it. I'm sorry that you had a bad experience, but let's put that behind us. Let's agree to be in regular communication about this progress. For the first couple of weeks, can we meet in person? We can get him right back on track." They could, and they did.

16. *Soft skills are developed and valued in our school.*

In general, soft skills are those that help someone interact in positive, pro-social, and even harmonious ways with other people. Soft skills often open doors to promotions, and they are critical during the interview process. The lack of soft skills puts people at risk for under- and unemployment. There is no official list of soft skills that students must develop, but here are some to consider:

- Communicating, verbally and nonverbally, with others.
- Demonstrating commitment and perseverance.
- Flexibility and adaptability, especially to stressful situations and changing demands.
- Time management and task monitoring.
- Leadership, taking responsibility for tasks, and motivating others.

- Creativity and problem-solving skills.
- Teamwork and collaborative efforts.

There certainly a number of valuable soft skills that we have left out, but you get the point. These skills are not clearly identified in any set of standards. Rather, they are habits that students need to develop to succeed in life. Schools provide students with the opportunity to practice and learn these soft skills.

The staff at Harbor Middle School is very focused on the development of soft skills for their students. As the principal noted, "When visitors come to our school, they are always impressed by the behaviors they see in our students. Visitors typically comment that these students are ready for adulthood and their careers. We have worked hard in identifying the types of skills that our students need and then building those needs into the flow of the classrooms."

These efforts were evident in visits to the classrooms at Harbor Middle. In one classroom, students were reminded to manage their time so that their tasks were complete. In another, students were working on a complex math problem that involved building a park and, when asked, said that they had been working on it for two days and that they believed that they were nearing completion of the project. Another group of students were working collaboratively and provided each other feedback on their contributions to the group. In every classroom we visited, evidence of the focus on soft skills was obvious.

Efforts to develop soft skills are not limited to adolescents. The staff at Harriet Tubman Elementary School identified specific soft skills that they wanted their students to practice at each grade level. For example, the primary grade teachers focused on turn taking, active listening, and asking topically related questions. The 3rd grade teachers focused on students' managing their materials, reaching agreements, sharing their opinions with others, and accepting and responding to criticism. This continued across the grade levels, with the school building a number of habits with their students.

For example, in Jason Harp's 5th grade classroom, students were working on a group project. They were reminded that they were working on their leadership skills, which included

- Seeking feedback from others.
- Maintaining a positive work environment.
- Following instructions and asking clarifying questions.
- Showing initiative.

When asked, every student in the room knew what these behaviors were and why they were important. They talked with a level of sophistication that was impressive. And every one of them qualified for free or reduced-price lunch. Across the years, their teachers at Tubman Elementary had built their soft skills so that they could interact with others in meaningful ways while remaining focused on the task at hand and maintaining strong relationships. These skills will serve them well in middle and high school and as they begin their careers, whether or not they enter college.

First Steps: It Starts with You

Individual teachers can do a lot to cultivate systems that support opportunity to learn. Begin by examining your classroom grouping practices. Do you regularly use a combination of whole-group and small-group instruction? Do you group both heterogeneously and homogenously? If you've been using the same grouping configurations for six weeks or more, change them up! We also recommend making attendance an agenda item in every meeting with parents, including back-to-school conferences and IEP meetings. (Remember that you don't have to be the one who runs the IEP meeting to put a topic on the agenda.) Finally, if schoolwide opportunity to learn data are not being captured and monitored in your school, consider giving the administration a nudge. Figure 3.1 shows a list of indicators that merit every school's attention.

FIGURE 3.1
Metrics to Monitor: Opportunity to Learn

✓ Graduation requirements

✓ Advanced course offerings and enrollments

✓ Transcript analyses to track for graduation and advanced diplomas

✓ Enrollment in key gateway courses (e.g., Algebra 1, College Preparatory English)

✓ Honors and Advanced Placement policies that might exclude students

✓ College admission testing and results for students in grades 8–12

✓ Specialized academic progress monitoring for students with disabilities, English learners, and any students at risk for failure

✓ Policies, practices, and procedures for creating class rosters

✓ Policies, procedures, and practices for in-grade retention of students

✓ Teacher collaboration schedules and results

Conclusion

It is a fiction to believe that all students have an equal opportunity to learn. The evidence clearly indicates that the Matthew principle—"the rich get richer, and the poor get poorer"—is alive and well, only this time, it's knowledge, not just money, that is the currency. Structural inequities, such as tracking and limited curricular options, constrain student growth. Other practices, such as in-grade retention, set into motion a trajectory of failure that plays out in slow motion across a child's academic career. But there is great hope in leveraging the human and social capital of our school and neighborhood communities. As educators, we need to be on the lookout for policies and procedure that, however well-intentioned they may be, serve as gates students must pass through in order to advance. Removal of these gates can expand every child's opportunity to learn. And isn't that what we're here to do?

CHAPTER 4

Instructional Excellence
Teach Well, and Students Will Learn

The students enrolled in Kennedy High School's three-year Career and Technical Education (CTE) program are seeing teaching from both sides of the desk. The work they're doing to develop the skills, knowledge, and dispositions of an educator includes coursework and 300 hours of internship fieldwork. These students are busy, attending regular high school academic classes in addition to their CTE courses dedicated to child development and instructional practices. They spend one day each week in classrooms at a nearby elementary school.

"I had no idea teachers worked so hard!" remarked Tasia. She was learning about lesson planning and instruction and had just finished teaching her first independent lesson to a small group of 1st grade math students. Tasia's lesson on the attributes of shapes had taken her an hour to prepare but only 15 minutes to teach. "It takes a lot to get them to pay attention," Tasia noted. "I'm glad I learned about using purpose statements to let them know what they'll be learning. All my own teachers use purpose statements, so that part was kind of natural." She explained that her work with the four 1st graders had given her new insight. "Now I really understand how going back to the purpose statement later in the lesson is a good way to keep their attention," she said. "And now I see why my teachers repeat that purpose statement again at the end. They want to know who learned it and who didn't. I'm going to watch my teachers closer now. I'm looking for good tips to use when I teach."

The previous chapters described elements in the Building Equity Taxonomy that create powerful conditions for addressing inequities in our schools and for increasing conditions for effective instruction and critical educational outcomes. As we address and improve on each of those elements, we must make sure we never lose sight of our instructional focus and commitment to instructional excellence. Without that, there can be no equity.

This chapter is about instructional excellence, with a focus on the lives of teachers and leaders. We will begin by discussing a framework for quality instruction, which includes differentiation and inclusive practices for students with disabilities. Next, we'll consider how grading and assessment affect teaching and learning, especially through compensatory and adaptive practices. Finally, we will spotlight the importance of professional learning to foster teacher expertise and leadership.

Why Instructional Excellence Is Important for Equity

Learning is at the heart of what schools do. This may seem obvious, but in too many schools, the distractions of discipline, sports, and infrastructure overwhelm the mission of the school. In equitable schools, leaders make certain that every system is aligned to support teaching and learning; those that interfere have to go. Certificated and clerical personnel need to understand that the work they do contributes directly to the learning of students. Finally, teachers need to balance discussion of teaching with examination of student learning. When the spotlight is only on the teacher, students sit by in the dark.

A Framework for Quality Teaching

All of us intend to be good at our work. We seldom encounter anyone in this profession who doesn't desire to perform effectively in his or her classroom. But how we talk with one another about quality is a different matter. Without a shared understanding of what quality looks like, we can't support one another.

If you are an instructional leader, coach, mentor, or supportive peer, you have probably encountered this reality. Without mutual agreements about quality instructional moves, people are impervious to your feedback. This is one reason much of our work has focused on creating a shared vocabulary, so that educators can understand one another when they talk about quality instruction and how to provide it. At our school, we reach agreements about quality instruction collaboratively, and our exploration of and decisions about these schoolwide practices are part collaborative decision making and part professional development. By engaging in this process, we build a sense of collective ownership and efficacy (Derrington & Angelle, 2013).

The result of our exploration and agreement has been a schoolwide commitment to practices drawn from an extensive research base in the learning sciences that transcend both content and grade level. One of the hallmarks is our use of *the gradual release of responsibility instruction framework*. First used by Pearson and Gallagher (1983) to describe reading comprehension, the gradual release of responsibility describes the cognitive and metacognitive shifts learners undergo as they move from acquisition to consolidation to transfer of knowledge (Fisher & Frey, 2014). This progression moves student learning forward through specific practices that begin with establishing purpose, and include teacher modeling, guided instruction, collaborative learning, independent learning, and formative evaluation of student learning throughout the process (see Figure 4.1). These are instructional moves, and as such, they should never be misinterpreted as being linear. Let's take a closer look at the model's various components and functions.

Focused instruction: Establishing purpose

Learners perform better when they know what they are learning, why they are learning it, and how they will know they have learned it. In fact, these three *what*, *why*, and *how* questions lurk in the minds of every student at every age. The practice of establishing the purpose for learning has long been understood to be a necessary component of a quality lesson. The practice goes by different names—learning targets, learning goals, learning intentions and success criteria, and objectives—but the fundamental concept is that

FIGURE 4.1

The Gradual Release of Responsibility Instructional Framework

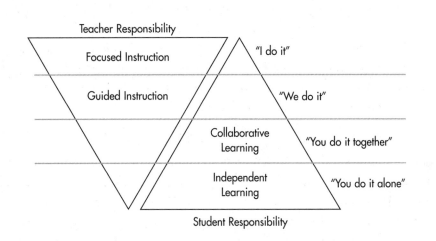

Source: From *Better Learning Through Structured Teaching: A Framework for the Gradual Release of Responsibility, 2nd edition* (p. 3), by D. Fisher and N. Frey, 2014, Alexandria, VA: ASCD. Copyright 2014 by ASCD.

learning expectations should be communicated clearly to students, revisited throughout the lesson, and used to provide formative feedback to the learner (Fisher & Frey, 2011).

The components of a purpose statement include the content, language, and social purposes for the lesson:

- The **content** portion isn't a standard (which is too broad) but is focused on the day's learning—a part of the standard that can be mastered within the lesson. This provides a bite-sized measure of a huge undertaking that might take days or weeks to master. For instance, informing 1st graders that the day's content purpose is to "ask questions of the main character in today's story" is more specific and, thus, more effective than informing them that they need to "produce and expand complete simple and compound declarative, interrogative, imperative, and exclamatory sentences in response to prompts."

- The **language** portion of the statement signals the vocabulary, syntax, or functions of language students will be using in the lesson. Extending our 1st grade example, the language purpose would be to "correctly use *who, what, when, where, why,* and *how* to pose questions."
- The **social purpose** portion addresses some of the social-emotional learning skills we referred to in Chapter 2. In our 1st grade example, it would be "We will listen to the ideas of others and take turns while speaking."

These purposes are usually conveyed both orally and in writing. For example, high school mathematics teacher Max Butler has been teaching exponential functions to his students over several weeks. In one lesson on applying these functions to different scenarios involving borrowing money to buy a car, his content purpose was "to use our understanding of exponential functions to make informed financial decisions," and his language purpose was "to infer mathematical meaning from the texts." His social purpose was "to make sense of complex problems within our small groups and persevere in solving them." He posted his purpose statements, discussed them with the class, and asked the students to record these statements in their math notebooks. It's a technique that contextualizes the information for students when they return to them days or weeks later to study them. In addition, Mr. Butler uses the purpose statements to support transitions (e.g., "Before you move to your table groups, remember that the purpose for learning today is…"). As the lesson draws to a close, he revisits the purpose statement so that students can engage in self-reflection about their progress toward goals. He might collect these self-reflections as exit slips and respond the next day with additional supports, re-teaching, or peer tutoring.

Focused instruction: Teacher modeling

When students are new to content, it helps to apprentice them into understanding how others make decisions about the associated skills and concepts. Teacher modeling with accompanying think-alouds shows students *how* a more expert person chooses a course of action. For example, the process of drawing inferences during reading can seem mysterious to students, leading them to conclude they are supposed to "just know" what every word means. Thinking aloud can help lift the veil. Here's an example, featuring 3rd grade teacher Serena Gannett, who read the following passage to her students:

> The organ pipe cactus grows in the Sonoran Desert. It is scorching hot in the day, and can dip below freezing at night. There is very little rain for the cactus to grow. But it is hardy. It doesn't need a nurse tree nearby to survive, like the saguaro cactus does.

Ms. Gannett then started thinking aloud:

> I'm not sure what *hardy* means. I can't write a definition of it. But I can infer its meaning. There are clues I am noticing. The first clue is in the sentence about the nurse tree: *It doesn't need a nurse tree.* I know that a nurse is someone who helps a person when they are sick or weak. So maybe a *nurse tree* is a tree that can protect a weak plant. I'm still not 100 percent sure, so I am also thinking about how hard it must be to live in the Sonoran Desert. The author said it is *scorching hot* in the daytime, and *freezing* at night. I can use what I know about plants to try to figure this out. Most plants don't grow well when it's too hot or too cold. But the organ pipe cactus is *hardy*. So I can infer that *hardy* means *tough*. This cactus is tough. It doesn't need a nurse tree to protect it, and it can grow even when it is very hot and very cold.

You can see that Ms. Gannett used several recommended techniques during this think-aloud. First, she used *I* statements to signal her own thinking ("But I can infer its meaning"), not *you* statements ("You can infer its meaning"). This is because the second-person *you* is directive, rather than invitational. Next, she engaged in speculation. Of course she really does know what *hardy* means, but she unpacked her thinking at the novice level, where her students are, to demonstrate how she draws an inference. As a fluent reader, she makes inferences subconsciously and in a split second. Here, though, she is slowing down the action for a few moments so her students can witness what just took place.

Think-alouds are brief in nature, lasting only a few minutes at most. But when students are learning a new skill or concept, putting things into slow motion is an effective way to familiarize them with the decision making involved. We promote think-alouds and all kinds of teacher modeling as instructional equity strategies because they increase student access to the curriculum.

Focused instruction: Noticing

The ability to notice learning is a factor that distinguishes expert teachers from novices (Donovan & Bransford, 2005). Notice we said expert, not *experienced* teachers. There are early-career teachers who are experts and teachers with 20 years of experience who are still novices. The observational skills employed by expert teachers as they make decisions about when to transition to guided instruction can be described as *noticing*. This is not as simple as determining whether a student's response is correct or not; it extends to being able to rapidly hypothesize what children know and do not know at a particular moment in time. It's when knowledge of how students learn really pays off. The term *expert blind spot* has been used to describe the phenomenon of novice teachers who understand their content but do not possess sufficient pedagogical content knowledge to foster learning (Nathan & Petrosino, 2003). Much has been written about noticing in teaching, with definitions centering on four facets of decision making (Huang & Li, 2012):

- Recognizing patterns across learners.
- Attending to salient information while disregarding unimportant events.
- Speculating and entertaining multiple possible reasons for student responses or misconceptions.
- Identifying a strategy to address the confusion.

Fifth grade teacher Hector Muniz is an expert teacher, as judged by his ability to use noticing in his practice. During a unit on decimals, Mr. Muniz noticed that many of his students were making errors when they transcribed an equation presented horizontally into one written on the vertical. He knew that a simple solution would be to review how problems should be set up. But more important, he recognized that the incorrect way students were aligning vertical equations signaled that they had only a partial understanding of the concepts behind decimals. The teacher realized that what the students needed was to revisit place value concepts. "I could have just told them to be careful to line up the decimals," he said. "That corrects the algorithm, but it doesn't address the conceptual understanding of quantity, which is what my next lessons are going to be about."

In short, noticing student performance in order to plan, adjust, and advance lessons is an equitable instructional practice because equitable instruction is responsive to student-demonstrated needs.

Guided instruction

At some point during the lesson, students need to try on new knowledge for themselves. Unfortunately, the practice of "I did it in front of you, now you do it alone by yourself" exposes a chasm that is just too challenging for many to breach. (In fact, if they can already do "it" after seeing it done once, you may have wasted time teaching students something they already knew how to do.) The unintended consequence of this approach is that it leaves students practicing incorrectly or inefficiently, thus habituating them to making errors.

Guided instruction is a way out of this trap—a technique that allows the teacher to share skills and information but also provide timely feedback in the form of questions, prompts, and cues to scaffold learning (Fisher & Frey, 2010). When a student is stuck, these techniques are ways to help bridge gaps in knowledge and enable action.

Questions are the logical place to begin, and they should be phrased to elicit as much information as possible so that the student gains a clear idea of what to do next:

- "Why do you think that is so?"
- "What are you trying to find?"
- "How did you get that result?"
- "Why does that work?"
- "Is there another way you can represent that result?"

There are times when questioning is sufficient, and the act of considering the question and answering aloud gives the student all the insight necessary to proceed. When questions aren't enough, a teacher should move to *prompts*, which help the student recall background or prior knowledge he or she has but has temporarily forgotten to apply:

- "What do you remember about states of matter?"
- "Remember the saying? *When two vowels go walking…* "
- "Take a look at our purpose statement for today. How can that help you?"

When questions and prompts don't move the student forward, *cues* may help. Cues are more overt, as they shift attention to sources of information. They might be

- **Physical**, such as offering hand-over-hand assistance to a young child printing his name.
- **Gestural**, as when pointing to the class word wall.
- **Environmental**, as when placing a language chart from a previous lesson near a student's table.
- **Verbal**, as when increasing or decreasing the rate or intonation of a prompt to emphasize a point. "And that's important *because…*"

It's important to stress that guided instruction doesn't occur exclusively during a designated part of the lesson. In many cases, guided instruction occurs intermittently throughout modeling, discussion, and collaborative or independent learning.

There's a difference between *not knowing* and *not knowing yet*. Providing scaffolding in the form of questions, prompts, and cues gives students the space and time they need to consolidate their thinking. When they are not able to do so, even after scaffolding, expert teachers go back to modeling and thinking aloud before releasing responsibility back to the learner. ("Now you try it.") Why do we identify the use of guided instruction as a substantial and equitable instructional practice? Because it requires teachers to make a thoughtful and informed plan to transition their specific, individual students from teacher-directed learning.

Collaborative learning

Learning is social (Vygotsky taught us that), and peers are an essential component in the equation. Collaborative learning occurs during the lesson when students work together to consolidate knowledge. Pushing four desks together and calling it collaborative learning won't work (we call that collaborative *seating*). Nor will assigning a task to a group and then watching them divide it up to work on it individually. The task needs to be sufficiently challenging such that they need one another to achieve success. The social-emotional and communication skills necessary for such endeavors can be a stretch for some students, especially as they attempt to resolve problems, disagree about ideas, and establish timelines for completion. Importantly, the language purposes for the lesson often invoke these skills. The speaking and listening standards are an invaluable guide for this facet of their learning.

We strive for collaborative learning to consume about 50 percent of instructional class time. That's a goal, not a mandate, but we feel that collaborative learning is the centerpiece of instruction and that it builds the kind of skills students need to function in their adult lives. The time spent on collaborative learning varies based on the time of year and the age of the students, of course. But because collaborative learning is so vital, the following understandings about quality collaborative learning are essential (Fisher & Frey, 2014):

- The tasks assigned accurately reflect the established purposes.
- Students use strategies and skills that were previously modeled.
- The task is appropriately complex. It is a novel application of a grade level–appropriate concept and is designed so that the outcome is not guaranteed (a chance for productive failure exists).
- Small groups of 2–5 students are purposefully constructed to maximize individual strengths without magnifying areas of need.

- Students use accountable talk to persuade, provide evidence, and ask questions of one another, and they disagree without being disagreeable. (pp. 139–140)

While students are engaged in collaborative learning, the teacher is actively working with groups of students. At any given time, the teacher might be scaffolding a group who is stuck by using questions, prompts, and cues, or by modeling and thinking aloud about a concept they are struggling with. This is a critical time for noticing, especially in seeing patterns across the class and determining what's important and what isn't. The result of this noticing might come in the form of pulling the groups back together to clarify information or even suspending collaborative learning altogether so that more direct teaching can take place. Collaborative learning is an instructional practice that promotes equity in our classrooms as it expands student engagement in the learning process and fosters a wide range of 21st century skills.

Independent learning

There's a reason we call for independent learning and not *independent practice*. That's because learning should deepen through independent application and extension. An essential goal of independent learning is to build fluent application of concepts and skills, especially by facilitating transfer of knowledge to increasingly novel situations. This has implications for homework. Too often, homework is used to complete the work the teacher ran out of time to teach in class—28 percent of teachers confessed to assigning this kind of homework on a regular basis (MetLife, 2007). But that doesn't make any sense. If the concept or skill is new, why would you expect that the student would be able to finish learning it alone, without guidance, hours later? Homework should be used to revisit previously learned concepts that are foundational to the unit of instruction, such as completing addition problems during an initial introduction to multiplication. A second purpose of homework is for fluency building, such as reading for 15 minutes each night.

Independent learning in and out of the classroom is an excellent opportunity for students to apply and extend their thinking. Digital environments are making it easier for students to engage in investigation, research, and writing. Many teachers have a parallel digital classroom where students post work, retrieve resources, and engage in discussion boards. However, lack of access exposes inequities for some schools and their students. Rural districts may lack the bandwidth needed to support the extensive use of technology, and poorer districts may lack the funds to purchase and maintain devices. The Schools and Library Program (commonly referred to as E-Rate) provides fiscal assistance to communities that face connectivity issues, and a variety of federal, state, and private funds are used to fund end-user hardware and software.

At the local level, some districts are transforming 1:1 technology initiatives into more supportive hybrid programs that allow students to link their own devices to school networks. However, the use of personal devices is viewed with suspicion by some educators who are concerned with possible misuse in classrooms. The answer isn't to ban such devices but rather to teach the kinds of digital citizenship skills needed. After all, not too long ago, educators dreamed of a computer for every student. In many quarters we have achieved that, but the devices are smartphones rather than school laptops and tablets. Students living in the 33 percent of American households with no broadband are increasingly using their smartphones to access the Internet, and the rate of doing so is increasing, especially among African Americans, rural residents, and those in families with incomes of less than $20,000 a year (Horrigan & Duggan, 2015). Knowing that a significant number of students are accessing the Internet using smartphones, it is critical that we consider how it is that students will complete assignments and research independently outside of school, and align our classroom practices so that we can teach them how to do so effectively.

No discussion of instructional excellence overlooks how we create access to learning in the classroom. We must also include information access outside of the classroom, and teach skills by leveraging the paths our students use. That means reexamining technology usage policies, selecting mobile-friendly apps, and modeling how they are used so that students can engage in meaningful independent learning. Systematically preparing students to work and learn independently is an important component of equitably preparing students with the skills they need to thrive as students and as global citizens.

Taking Instructional Excellence Schoolwide

A challenge with raising the bar on instructional excellence is one of scale. In conventional school settings, there is an unspoken assumption that what occurs in a classroom is essentially a private act. This belief contributes to a kind of stagnation of practice. Working in isolation from peers, novice teachers have little opportunity to gain expertise, and seasoned teachers may work for years without ever becoming experts.

Schoolwide practices—agreements about providing certain foundational experiences for all students—can open doors and promote meaningful collaboration among teachers, helping them to expand their instructional palettes and goals. An additional benefit of adopting and implementing schoolwide instructional practices is that it signals to the entire community—staff, students, and families—what is valued academically. This congruence between the stated values and the behaviors of an organization build a sense of *collective teacher efficacy*, which is a group of educators' perception that they have the capacity to positively affect the academic performance of their students (Goddard, Hoy, & Woolfolk Hoy, 2000).

Three of us worked for many years with a large urban high school in San Diego that used schoolwide practices as a means to transform student learning and instructional excellence (Fisher, Frey, & Williams, 2002). One hundred percent of the students in this majority-minority school qualified for free or reduced-price lunch. Teachers and administrators at the school regularly met to review research on effective instructional strategies and discuss which ones had a universal application across grade levels and disciplines. In time, we arrived at agreement on seven defensible strategies: read-alouds and shared readings, graphic organizers, K-W-L charts, writing-to-learn approaches, vocabulary instruction, structured note taking, and reciprocal teaching. Through these professional learning sessions, we all focused on building new skills. To support these efforts, the school scheduled collegial coaching partnerships to encourage more classroom consultations and collaboration among peers. We had insight into what we were doing, and we spurred one another to greater success.

We also noticed how our students' familiarity with these seven strategies streamlined instruction; there was no need to devote lots of time to how to use graphic organizers, for example, or reciprocal teaching, because these were schoolwide practices.

A schoolwide literacy compact served the entire organization. Within two years, the school met its state accountability targets for the first time in 15 years. In five years, the average reading level of students in grades 9–12 had risen by 2.4 years, and the school posted the largest accountability measure gains in the city (Fisher et al., 2002). To be sure, this took lots of hard work on the part of teachers, coaches, and administrators. But their commitment to the schoolwide agreements—plus the addition of structural supports that bolstered both student learning and teachers' professional learning—stabilized a school that had previously been in flux.

That's not to say that every school has to agree to implement the seven instructional strategies that our school did. We have since been involved in other efforts to create schoolwide practices that have involved different and fewer approaches (e.g., Fisher, Frey, & Lapp, 2009). What we have learned is that schoolwide approaches work because they develop two things:

- **Transparency**, meaning that the approach (such as Cornell note taking) becomes a habit students use rather than a novelty in some classes and not others. When the strategy or routine becomes transparent, students can focus more on *what* is being taught than on *how* it is being taught.
- **Transportability**, meaning that the approach is used often enough and in different enough contexts that students learn how to vary the approach and assume ownership of it. Returning to the idea of note

taking, when students use this approach in different classes, they learn how to adjust the system accordingly.

No, implementing transportable and transparent instructional routines for students does not mean that teachers become robots who just follow a script. There is a lot of skill involved in using these tools, but there is an art to it, too. The point is not to control teachers but to make school a little more predictable for students. It's about providing a degree of consistency across the day and across school years.

Systems to Support Instructional Excellence

In Chapter 3's discussion of opportunity to learn, we discussed the importance of creating school structures (e.g., course offerings, class rosters, and curriculum) to build needed human and social capital. Our concern here is extending those opportunities by ensuring that quality instruction takes place throughout the building. However, these efforts can quickly erode without the compensatory and adaptive instructional practices necessary to support such structures. That is why we consider these practices as essential components of creating and advancing equitable access to our curriculum. It is one thing to restructure in order to create more opportunities to learn. But we can't stand by and wait for a critical mass of "qualified students" to somehow appear. The students we have now—today—are the students we need to serve.

It's obviously magical thinking to believe that simply renaming a school "The Academy of Little Madame Curies and Isaac Newtons" is going to transform the children learning there into budding physicists and mathematicians, but many well-intentioned restructuring efforts have naively subscribed to a similar "if we build it, they will come" school of thought. Weis and colleagues (2015) followed the efforts of eight urban high schools serving poor and ethnic minority students, each of which restructured in order to offer more challenging curriculum. But within three years, these efforts dissipated because the schools could not sustain the courses due to low enrollment. These comments from a counselor at one of the high schools sum up the problem:

> I mean, you have your occasional 11th grader—I can think of two right now—who are math whizzes, but you are talking about two [students] in the whole class. You can't have two [students] in a class, and it is unfortunate because then those two kids in every grade miss out. We don't have a statistics course for fourth year because there are just no bodies to put in there. (p. 1045)

The fatal flaw, from our perspective, was failing to put other structures in place to scaffold student learning so that all students would be "qualified" to take on the challenging curriculum. Although the counselor noted that there were two "math whizzes" in the grade level, the school she worked at couldn't see that there were 100 more with potential. We have to grow our own math whizzes, critical thinkers, deep readers, engineering geniuses, and brilliant writers. That means that we need to actively build compensatory practices, especially tutoring and mentoring, to accelerate students' knowledge acquisition. In addition, we must build our collective capacity to use adaptive learning approaches, especially differentiation and inclusive practices, to effectively support all the students in every class.

Compensatory practices

As we have stressed, equality should not be confused with equity. Students arrive at the schoolhouse doors with a range of strengths, interests, motivations, and gaps. To somehow expect that each student will possess the prerequisite knowledge, skills, and dispositions he or she needs to fully benefit from challenging curriculum is a fool's game. And it's a dangerous game, too, because it perpetuates a belief that school is a hierarchical system intent on stratifying students into those who are more and less able. It perpetuates a false meritocracy that provides more rewards to those who already have more, while those who have less continue to get less.

Fully anticipate that instituting a more challenging curriculum paired with quality instruction will mean putting in place compensatory tutoring and academic recovery systems. By all means, offer (and fill) advanced courses with the students you have, but also expect that a number of these students will struggle without appropriate support.

We've written about the tutoring and academic recovery efforts at the middle and high school where we work and how these are tied to grading policies (Fisher, Frey, & Pumpian, 2011, 2012). We use a competency-based grading system schoolwide. Grades are calculated based on mastery of competency assessments, such as unit tests and performance-based culminating projects. Students are not graded on homework completion, classroom participation, or bringing a pencil to class. (We do think all of those behaviors are important, so we report on them separately as representations of citizenship.) Students who do not pass a competency assessment at 70 percent or better receive an "incomplete," not a failing grade, much as they would in college. Teachers at our school digitally sweep our electronic grade books every Sunday to identify each student with an incomplete by class and by date, and the incomplete triggers a cascade of compensatory practices.

The first level of compensatory practice occurs during a student meeting with the teacher to formulate a plan. Tutorials in every discipline are available before and after school, as well as during lunch each day, and students are required to complete the practice work (readings, homework, etc.) assigned for the unit in question. (Teachers do assign homework; they just don't calculate it into the grade.) Once the practice work is completed, the student is eligible to take an alternate form of the competency assessment. They have two weeks to "clear" the incomplete grade on their own.

If the student has not cleared the grade in two weeks, this triggers a second level of compensatory practice: a meeting (often by phone) of the student, the teacher, and a parent to develop a more formal plan. This plan usually involves mandatory attendance at tutorials, which are staffed by teachers and peer tutors.

Over a decade of doing this, we can affirm in no uncertain terms that families are uniformly supportive of this process and are relieved that their child is getting the help he or she needs, even if sometimes the student is not so grateful. Most students are able to clear their incompletes through the first or second levels of support.

We would be remiss if we subscribed only to a "wait to fail" model of support. Therefore, our school reserves a third level of compensatory practices for students who are already behind even before they begin. At the beginning of each school year, we comb standards-based assessment results and screening tools to identify students who will need more comprehensive support in order to successfully complete their coursework. Every student has an additional period on his or her schedule, immediately after the end of the regular school day. Many use it for general homework and study supports, and students who need compensatory services might be scheduled for English language development instruction, tutoring to close gaps in subject matter knowledge, or additional instruction based on past performance. Because this time slot is on everyone's schedule, families and students know that this is still part of the school day. Clubs and sports are scheduled to begin after this period ends so that no one has conflicts.

In their junior and senior years, students can enroll in community college courses that are primarily taught onsite, with the exception of a few that require specialized lab facilities. College instructors teach their courses in the presence of a student support staff member. After the college course class meeting ends, students attend a study lab run by assigned high school personnel. The 90-minute period is used to reinforce content, to provide additional aid for readings and homework, and to prepare for quizzes and tests. In other words, we provide high school supports for college classes. Our hope is to reinforce for these students that postsecondary success requires more than seat time in class, and that building a habit of seeking out study group opportunities affords many supports that cannot be acquired during college lectures.

One other important compensatory practice is mentoring. Every school year, we meet students who need extra support and guidance. You've met them throughout your educational careers; they're the ones who just need someone to be there for them. They draw your attention because they are boisterous, or loud, or silly, or sullen, or silent. As an administrative team, we have enacted a procedure that, quite frankly, is a secret from the kids. We solicit input from teachers and student support personnel during the first week of school about those students who need a bit more of *something*. We take the list of students, divide it among ourselves, and take on the task of building a relationship with these kids. We talk to "our" kids every day, whether they like it or not, about everything under the sun—except for school. *What bands do you like? What did you think about the basketball game last night? I keep hearing that I should read that book you're holding. What do you think of it?* When you engage in this way, it doesn't matter what you say—just that you know these students' names and you talk to them every day. They don't ever need to know why they were noticed. They just need to know someone is there for them. Relationships grow.

Adaptive practices

The compensatory practices discussed in the previous section occur primarily outside of core classroom instructional time, and are intended to close knowledge gaps and noncognitive gaps that hinder academic success. But supports also need to be available inside the classroom. A substantial part of this support comes from using a gradual release of responsibility instructional framework to support learning. But concomitant to the framework are *differentiation* and *inclusive practices*.

Differentiation. Tomlinson (2014) describes a differentiated classroom as a place where teachers

> provide specific alternatives for individuals to learn as deeply as possible and as quickly as possible, without assuming one student's road map for learning is identical to anyone else's. These teachers believe that students should be held to high standards. They work diligently to ensure that all students work harder than they meant to; achieve more than they thought they could; and come to believe that learning involves risk, error, and personal triumph. These teachers also work to ensure that all students consistently experience the reality that success stems from hard and informed work. (p. 7)

Can't you hear the student empowerment? It comes through attention to three facets of the classroom experience: content, process, and product (Tomlinson, 2014). Differentiation is not about providing different assignments for lots of different students. Rather, it requires attention to student goal setting, as the teacher crafts a plan for learning with students such that their path is mutually understood. In too many classes, students adopt a passive stance because the teacher determines the path, and it's the same for everyone. Differentiation requires that students know what the destination is, and with the teacher's guidance, they work to accomplish their learning goals.

Inclusive practices. This term encompasses a number of important structures that can support the collaborative work of general and special educators and ensure that students with and without disabilities are educated together. For example, in the middle school where he works, Angelo Matapang, an inclusion support specialist, does not operate a self-contained classroom. Instead, he moves from class to class, focusing on supporting students and collaborating with fellow teachers.

The supports he provides are designed around three elements: (1) assistive and augmentative technologies, (2) curricular accommodation and modifications, and (3) personal supports. The last of these, personal supports, are absolutely vital, and they range across a continuum from most intensive to least intensive (Fisher & Frey, 2003):

- **Full-time support** is where a staff person remains in close proximity to offer physical assistance throughout the day. Full-time support staff rotate throughout the day so that the child experiences a wider range of social and communication experiences. Each staff member is knowledgeable about the curriculum.
- **Part-time support** by a staff person is provided at scheduled times, such as during a music class, but not for the entire day. The staff person is knowledgeable about the curriculum.
- **Intermittent support** is delivered by a peer or paid staff person to troubleshoot specific situations. Curriculum expertise is not required.

- **Peer tutors** provide same-age or cross-age supports for a child, including mobility, note taking, and some curricular support.
- **Natural supports** emerge from the classroom and are fostered by the teacher through development of relationships and friendships. Every child, with or without a disability, relies on this form of support.
- **Supplemental supports** are delivered by related services personnel (e.g., speech-language pathologist, occupational therapist) within the classroom to generalize skills.

"We've learned a lot—through trial and error, I'd say—about personal supports," Mr. Matapang stated. He described mistakes from years ago when a student with significant disabilities was assigned to one paraprofessional all day. "The first time Ms. Carrillo was absent, we realized that none of us knew very well how to support the child," he said. "Ms. Carrillo was the only one who did. When we had a meeting with the family a few weeks later, the mother told us having a full-time, one-to-one staff member was the wrong way to go with her child, because it limited his communication."

Mr. Matapang explained that the school learned not to rely on personal supports to the exclusion of the curricular and technology tools available. "When we have a problem now, our problem-solving protocol is to examine all three categories of supports and make changes as needed in each of those categories," he said. "We look at those annually to design supports, sure," he said. "But you can't forget about fading. The supports some kids need at the beginning of the year can be faded as they develop skills. We want them to participate in and learn from the general education curriculum, but we have a sign in our conference room where we hold the IEPs," he said. "It says 'OASAN. Only as special as necessary.' We're always looking for growth."

Professional Learning

The instructional practices profiled in this chapter, from the gradual release of responsibility instructional framework to the compensatory and adaptive practices that support the framework, don't simply emerge by decree.

Teachers and support staff need and deserve ongoing professional learning. And it can't just be a big-group session where concepts are presented by an expert to the entire staff. Effective professional learning moves beyond "designated PD time" to include follow-up coaching, collaboration with fellow teachers, and examination of student work through professional learning communities.

An aggressive and focused commitment to professional learning demonstrates a willingness to commit resources to advancing equitable practices. The National School Board Association and the Center for Public Education issued a joint technical report on professional learning as a tool to effect change (Gulamhussein, 2013). In it, they make a case for regarding professional learning in two ways: as methods for developing teachers as technicians and as approaches for developing teachers as intellectuals. These organizations argue that the development of evidence-based teaching skills—the technical aspects of instruction—is an important element of learning that is best attended to through successive series of workshops and follow-up coaching. The best way to attend to teachers' intellectual development is through professional learning communities, where teachers engage in "an inquiry process where teachers innovate... examine broad research on learning and develop innovative classroom strategies to achieve goals" (Gulamhussein, 2013, p. 20).

Professional learning, therefore, is best seen not as an event in time but as a process that unfolds across a career. We created a teacher growth and leadership framework (see Fisher, Frey, & Hite, 2016) that parallels much of the work addressed in this book. There are five components to our Framework for Intentional and Target Teaching (or FIT Teaching) approach:

1. **Planning with purpose** through analysis of standards to determine purpose, success criteria, and transfer of skills.
2. **Cultivating a learning climate** by creating a welcoming climate that fosters learning and development.
3. **Instructing with intention** using the gradual release of responsibility instructional model.

4. **Assessing with a system** using formative assessment to take action.
5. **Impacting student learning** by using short- and long-term outcomes of instruction to gauge one's effectiveness.

We believe these components frame the work of teachers and should be leveraged to promote professional growth and leadership. As noted, we believe educators have a critical role to play in their own learning and in the learning lives of their colleagues, and we have translated the FIT Teaching approach into a tool that teachers can use to identify where they are at different points in their career and how they can develop further. Notably, the tool's level designations are linked not to experience but to expertise (Fisher, Frey, & Hite, 2016):

- **Not Yet Apparent.** This level is indicated only when there is a *complete lack of evidence* that the teacher has considered a necessary aspect of instruction and incorporated it into practice. This level should be differentiated from Not Applicable (NA), which indicates a rare situation when the ingredient is not expected as part of the teacher's practice.
- **Developing.** Most typical with teachers new to the profession or new to a grade level, subject area, or curriculum implementation, this level is marked by inconsistency of practice. It is selected by the teacher when it is clear that he or she understands the criteria but is having trouble with implementation.
- **Teaching.** Most typical with teachers experienced in implementing criteria with fidelity, this level is selected when it is clear to the teacher that his or her practice is intentional, solidly implemented, and resulting in success for students.
- **Leading.** This level is selected by the teacher who has embraced a particular aspect of the criterion at its highest level and is providing support, guidance, and resources for colleagues. *Leading* teachers develop learning opportunities for adults that respect individual levels of personal practice and focus on extending collective growth. Teachers at this level have classrooms with open doors and consider themselves continuous learners, thereby affecting classrooms outside their own.

We encourage teachers to use the FIT Teaching Tool primarily as a self-assessment and then to meet with other colleagues and administrators to plot goals for advancement in teacher leadership. Its intended use is not evaluation but the development and support of technical and intellectual prowess. It captures the reality that instructional excellence doesn't begin at the front of the classroom; it lives in the process of internalizing the habits of mind associated with powerful and effective educators.

Building Equity Review Statements: Instructional Excellence

This chapter has focused on the type of teaching that every student deserves. It has also looked at the instructional systems that need to be in place for students to achieve at high levels. As we have noted before, you can have a building full of diverse students and work to engage them and ensure opportunity to learn, but then you have to teach them well so that they *will* learn.

We'll turn now to guiding statements on the BER focused on aspects of instruction that can ensure equitable outcomes for all students and examples of what the work to achieve this looks like in schools.

17. All students experience quality core instruction.

A significant portion of this chapter has focused on quality core instruction. We are not going to repeat that information here, but we do want to reinforce that students must have access to instruction that builds both their confidence and their competence. Our experience and research suggest that teachers can accelerate learning when they

- State a clear learning intention or purpose for the lesson.
- Model their thinking and demonstrate their problem-solving strategies.
- Engage students in collaborative learning.
- Check for understanding on a regular basis.
- Guide students' understanding using prompts, cues, and questions.
- Hold students accountable for learning through independent tasks.
- Use student work to guide future instruction.

This looks fairly straightforward, and yet there are still a lot of students who are not provided with these kinds of learning experiences or the scaffolds necessary to succeed with them. For example, when we met middle school science teacher Anna Hargrove, she regularly assigned students significant amounts of independent work and did not use any collaborative learning techniques in her classroom. The majority of her students performed well on state tests, but those students who did the best had also performed well the year before (and probably the year before that). Ms. Hargrove's class relied on a significant practice effect—all of that independent work—but there was not much scaffolding for students who had not previously mastered the content. The equity issue was clear. Students who generally understood the scientific concepts before they met Ms. Hargrove did just fine working on their own. However, those who came to Ms. Hargrove's class without the conceptual understandings they could apply in independent work did not thrive with this instructional approach.

Ms. Hargrove was enrolled in a graduate class that required her to engage in collaborative action research, and her team voted to focus on productive group work and determining how to increase students' use of academic language. During their first meeting, team members were supposed to share work samples from a recent group task that they had assigned. Ms. Hargrove did not have anything to share. She confessed to the group that she rarely engaged her students in this type of learning. As she said that evening, "I'm not sure that I even know how to have students work together. If any of you have ideas, I'll try it out so that we can do this project." They did have ideas, and Ms. Hargrove did go on to try them out with her classes.

During the next meeting of the action research team, members talked about the outcomes each of them had achieved, and several of them noted that they had used argumentation sentence frames to help students interact with one another. Ms. Hargrove was interested, and asked to see them. She went on to try this strategy in her own class as well.

Over the course of the semester, Ms. Hargrove's class transformed. She started getting e-mails from parents saying how much their children were enjoying science. The overall grade point average of her students increased, and all but three students passed with a *C* or better. As Ms. Hargrove said, "I used to think that I would have to sacrifice my higher-achieving students to play catch-up with those who weren't excelling. But really, I was losing even the high achievers. They were compliant with my demands and did well, but they just weren't interested in science. Now, [after incorporating productive group work and a focus on academic language,] they're totally engaged and I have time to work closely with students who need me. Everyone is a doing a lot better as a result."

18. *There are transparent and transportable instructional routines in place schoolwide.*

Thinking about transportable and transparent instructional routines involves exploring the tension between predictability and monotony. We all expect and appreciate some predictability in our lives. It makes things easier when the coffee machine is in the same place every morning; having to search for it every day would decrease our productivity and increase our frustration. On the other hand, if everything were always completely predictable, life could become pretty boring. To varying degrees, people appreciate spontaneity and variety, and we tend to pay more attention when things are changed up a bit. But there is a limit to that. If everything is different every time, it's hard to detect patterns or engage in critical and creative thinking. In other words, predictability and novelty need to be in balance.

Our concern is that, for many students, every day and every hour within the day is novel. As a result, they are never sure what is expected of them, and they spend precious cognitive resources on how they are supposed to learn at any given moment. If they are strategic thinkers, they know that they will probably not be asked to learn this way again for some time. For schools to become equitable places for learning, there have to be some predictable routines that students can learn and follow.

"What are you willing to do, or sacrifice, to ensure that all students learn at high levels?" That was the question Principal Marco Juarez asked the teachers at Avondale Elementary School. The school had no common routines. Every teacher did what he or she wanted. Mr. Juarez continued, "I'm wondering if there are things that we could do to build students' habits so that we're not spending so much time focused on what we want them to do and are spending more time on what we want them to learn."

Over the course of the next several professional learning events, teachers in various grade levels agreed on some specific routines that they believed were developmentally appropriate. One of the major areas of agreement was vocabulary. They agreed to name concepts, starting in kindergarten, based on the technical name used in the standards. As a 1st grade teacher said, "No more saying, 'It is a describing word.' We're going to use *adjective* from now on. And no more 'action words'; we're going to say *verb*. If we all do this, they'll learn the correct terminology and the upper-grade teachers won't have to spend so much time re-teaching the labels for the concepts."

The teachers at Avondale also agreed to specific grade-level collaborative learning routines. As a 3rd grade teacher said, "If we really do this, the students I get next year will have some habits for interaction regardless of which 2nd grade teacher they had. That will save me so much time. This year, they all had different ways for working together, so I stopped and taught my ways. It really was a waste of time."

At Avondale, grade-level teams were asked to focus on two to four collaborative routines. The 2nd grade teachers settled on the following three.

Numbered heads together. The class is set up in small groups, and each group is assigned a number. Each student within the group is assigned (or selects) a number 1 through 4 (or 5, as numbers necessitate). The teacher asks a question and asks the groups to come up with answer, reminding them to make sure that every student in the group can answer. After students have time to discuss, the teacher spins the overhead spinner and announces the number of the student who will answer ("Student 3!"). Groups have one more minute to make sure this student in their group knows the answer. Then the teacher repeats the question, spins again, and announces the number of the group that must respond ("Group 2, you're up!"). Student 3 from Group 2 answers the question.

Four corners. The teacher assigns each corner of the room a category related to the lesson topic. After explaining the four categories, the teacher asks students to write down which category they are most interested in and two or three reasons why. At the teacher's signal, students go to their chosen corner, forming four interest-based groups. Then they share their reasons for choice. This routine is also an effective way to form groups to complete particular tasks.

Think-write-pair-share. The teacher gives students a minute to *think* about a prompt and then a few minutes to *write* down their ideas (typically in bullet or note form without focus on spelling or grammar). Students share their ideas in self-selected or assigned *pairs*, listening carefully to what their partner is saying. Then the teacher calls on a few pairs to *share* what their partners said with the whole class.

This approach of Avondale's may not seem like a big deal until you consider how long it takes 7-year-olds to master interactive routines. But as the Avondale teachers learned, once students develop these habits, you can expect them to get to work more quickly. And teachers the following year can count on these tools being available. As a 3rd grade teacher at Avondale noted, "Next year, all of my incoming students will know how to work together in three ways. Our grade level will add three more. But in a few years, all of the 3rd graders who come to me will know nine ways of working together because they'll have learned three collaborative routines in kindergarten, 1st grade, and 2nd grade."

Another teacher commented, "I don't love all of the choices my grade level agreed on, but I'm going to do them because I think that this is a really good plan for helping all our students succeed. I also will probably add one more, my personal favorite, which is reader's theater. It's not on our list as an option, so I hope that's OK." Her colleagues agreed that she should take this on, since this was important to her.

That's the power of transparent and transportable instructional routines. They build habits but they don't have to constrain teachers. Many years ago, a high school where we worked asked all teachers to build students' habits in taking Cornell notes. Not everyone was thrilled about this. Some people preferred outlining, and others preferred visual/graphic notes. But the majority of teachers agreed to use Cornell notes because their peers asked them to.

The proof came when graduates returned to visit and told us how well they were doing in college. "Most of the people in my history class didn't know how to take notes," one said. "Their notes were all random. When I'm in class, I just use the Cornell notes that we all learned here, and I review them, just like we learned, and then I write my summary later after I have reread the notes. A lot of people ask to take pics of my notes, which is fine, but I know that it's taking the notes and studying from them that helps me learn. I got an *A* in that history class, by the way."

19. *Grading and progress reports are focused on subject matter mastery and competence.*

Too often, the grades students receive reflect a mix of compliance and understanding, and the percentage that each contributes to students' grades varies across teachers, schools, districts, and states. This is problematic for students and their families, and it calls college admission decisions into question. In some schools, homework compliance contributes 50 percent of the grade. In other schools, 10 percent of the grade is based on homework. Thus the student who does none of the homework yet aces the test would fail in one school and earn a *B* in the other. That is, the student could have demonstrated mastery learning but earned an unsatisfactory grade.

This stands in stark contrast to what grades should do. While there are many who question the value of grades, especially when they are used to bribe students to complete work (e.g., Kohn, 1999), when grades are given, they should reflect students' understanding of the content. Grades are abbreviated information about a student's performance in a specific subject and should reflect a level of mastery of the content taught. To ensure that grades reflect competence rather than compliance, teachers have to design assessments that allow them to identify which students have demonstrated mastery.

We call these types of assessments *competencies*. Given that there is a wide range of ways for determining student understanding (Popham, 2011), teachers can develop a broad set of measures of competence. Some might be traditional tests consisting of multiple-choice and short-answer items. In addition, competencies might involve oral presentations, projects, performances, and writing. Here's a sample of the competencies used in our high school:

- A 20-page graphic novel retelling the events of the French Revolution, either inked by the student or using imported images.
- A 1,500-word essay and a creative component (such as an iMovie or original song) in response to the essential question "What is worse, failing or never trying?"
- A 25-item exam on polynomials with written explanations of the problem-solving procedures used for 10 of them.
- The development of a crime story in which the crime is solved using knowledge of DNA, RNA, and genetics.

This system works well for middle and high schoolers. At the elementary level, a competency-based approach calls for students to be evaluated against the standards and for teachers to issue progress reports that reflect individual levels of mastery. For example, the students in Amal Noor's 4th grade class are evaluated each trimester on the standards that have been taught. Ms. Noor keeps evidence for each student and reviews this with parents at their meetings. Figure 4.2 shows Jose's report card. Notice that there are several areas that have yet to be taught. There are also areas in which Jose has demonstrated mastery and other areas that need attention. The report card also includes learner qualities (especially the soft skills that we discussed in Chapter 3). This type of information, and the evidence used to draw these conclusions, helps Ms. Noor plan future instruction for Jose and provides his parents with information about his successes and challenges. The principal can review all report cards generated for trends and then identify professional learning needs for teachers and interventions for students.

20. Teachers notice students' individual instructional needs and have systems to differentiate as needed.

As we have discussed, expert teachers notice when their students have mastered a concept and when they need additional support to accomplish the learning goal. Noticing is essential, but it is what teachers do with the

FIGURE 4.2

Jose's Report Card

STUDENT	Jose Alvarado
GRADE	4
TEACHER	Amal Noor

READING

	Trimester I	II	III
Foundational Skills			
Phonics & word recognition	3		
Fluency (accuracy & fluency to support comprehension)	3		
Literature			
Key ideas & details	3		
Craft & structure	2		
Integration of knowledge & ideas	2		
Informational Text			
Key ideas & details	3		
Craft & structure	2		
Integration of knowledge & ideas	2		

WRITING

	Trimester I	II	III
Text Types & Purposes			
Opinion	2		
Informative	3		
Narrative	X		
Production & Distribution of Writing	2		
Research to Build & Present Knowledge	2		

LANGUAGE

	Trimester I	II	III
Conventions of Standard English			
Conventions of grammar	2		
Capitalization, punctuation, & spelling	3		
Knowledge of Language	2		
Vocabulary Acquisition & Use	2		

SPEAKING & LISTENING

	Trimester I	II	III
Comprehension & Collaboration	3		
Presentation of Knowledge & Ideas	2		

MATHEMATICS

	Trimester I	II	III
Operation & Algebraic Thinking	2		
Number & Operations in Base Ten	2		
Number & Operations—Fractions	2		
Measurement & Data	3		
Geometry	X		

SCIENCE

	Trimester I	II	III
Physical, Earth & Space, Life, Construct of Inquiry	3		

SOCIAL STUDIES

	Trimester I	II	III
Civics & Government, Historical Perspectives, Economics, Geography	2		

LEARNING QUALITIES

	Trimester I	II	III
Self-Directed			
Shows effort	c		
Organizes time, tasks, & materials	s		
Completes classwork on time	s		
Actively listens & responds	c		
Shows responsibility	c		
Produces work that is neat & organized	*		
Cooperative			
Works collaboratively in groups of various	c		
Works to achieve group goals	c		
Shares & receives information & ideas	c		

LEARNER QUALITIES

	Trimester I	II	III
Respectful			
Demonstrates respect for property, self, & others	c		
Follows school/classroom procedures	c		
Resolves conflict appropriately	c		
Accepts responsibility for actions	c		

ABSENCES/TARDINESS

Approximately 60 school days per reporting period.

	Trimester I	II	III	Total
Days Absent	2			2
Absences are affecting progress				
Days Tardy	1			1
Tardiness is affecting progress				

Performance Levels for Core Content, Co-Curricular Areas, & Learner Qualities

5	Exceeds Standard or Expectation
4	Mastery Attained
3	Developing Mastery
2	Initial or Beginning level of Mastery
1	Little or No Mastery
*	Needs Improvement
c	Consistently (Learner Quality)
s	Sometimes/Progressing (Learner Quality)
n	Needs Attention/Progressing (Learner Quality)
x	Not Assessed This Trimester

information that they have noticed that really makes a difference. In some cases, students may need to be retaught. In other cases, they may need to be challenged. In still other cases, they may need to spend more time in a group, struggling productively with a problem. There is no automatic way for teachers to respond to students' misunderstandings and errors. This is where instructional skill really lies: in teachers responding in the right way as the learner continues to learn.

Another sign of instructional skill is knowing that taking responsibility back from the learner and telling him or her the answer can do harm. In fact, there are a lot of students who have developed learned helplessness because the well-meaning adults in their lives simply told them the answers when they didn't know. Effective teachers guide students' learning past incorrect answers, and they do this via whole-class, small-group, and individual inter-actions. We think it's easier to guide students' learning if you can get them into smaller groups. But then you have to figure out what to do with the rest of the class. In part, we advocate for collaborative learning because it allows students opportunities to practice and develop academic language, but we also like how it provides teachers with an opportunity to meet with smaller groups of students.

The students in Christy Murphy's 3rd grade class were working collab-oratively, reading an informational text about life cycles. Ms. Murphy circu-lated in the room, checking in with groups to ensure that they understood the task and were engaged in collaborative conversations. She then invited four students to step away from their respective groups and meet her at the table in the front of the room. As they arrived, Ms. Murphy said, "I'm very excited to continue our conversation from yesterday. Have you all given any thought to the question I asked you at the end of our time together?"

Alex was the first to respond. "Yeah," he said, "I asked three people—my dad, my cousin, and my aunt—to tell me one thing that had a life cycle. I got three of them: trees, ducks, and goldfish."

Each student shared the three examples of items with a life cycle with the group while Ms. Murphy wrote down all of their answers. She then asked students to think about ways to sort the different ideas that they had generated. Brianna said, "Some of them are plants. We could make a category for plants."

Hector added, "And lots of them live in the water. We could make a category for things that live in the water, like frogs, ducks, and goldfish."

As the lesson continued, the students talked about what the things in each category had in common. They ended up changing the category of "things that live in the water" and grouped them instead by animal type: mammals, fish, birds, reptiles, and amphibians. As their time together came to an end, Ms. Murphy said, "So, for today's exploration, I'd like each of you to take one category and investigate what all of the examples in the category have in common in terms of their life cycle. In other words, I'm looking for the stages within the life cycle for each category. And it has to fit all of the examples within the category, OK?"

As these four students returned to their groups, Ms. Murphy invited three different students to join her at the table. As they sat down, she greeted them and said, "I am very excited to continue our conversation from yesterday. Have you all given any thought to the question I asked you at the end of our time together?"

Roberto was the first to answer. "My dad said that a life cycle is how it changes from when it's born to when it grows up," he said.

Betsy commented, "My mom and grandma didn't know so we searched online. My mom read it to me, and I remember that frogs start as eggs and then get to be tad… tad… tad-something. I forget!"

Their conversation continued, with Ms. Murphy building students' background knowledge and vocabulary. She elicited information from the students and used it to guide their thinking and their understanding.

The two groups were different in terms of their needs, but each received effective learning support from their teacher via guided instruction. Ms. Murphy designed her small-group interactions with students to address the learning gaps that she had identified.

Differentiation is another system teachers can use to ensure instruction will meet individual student needs. As we have noted, teachers can differentiate content, process, or products, and they can tailor these aspects of instruction to address student readiness, interests, and learning preferences. Differentiation is a more proactive approach, whereas the guided instruction that Ms. Murphy used was reactive. One is not better than the other; they are simply different systems that support equitable learning outcomes.

When we say differentiation is proactive, we mean that it is carefully planned, fueled by ongoing formative evaluation of students' performance and feedback to learners. To truly differentiate, teachers must pre-assess students to determine what they already know and do not know. Arlette Montgomery does this regularly with her 6th grade social studies students. Before introducing a unit of instruction, she administers a questionnaire about the content. In advance of a unit comparing the processes, rules, and laws in ancient China, Japan, and India, for example, these might be questions about civil service, samurai, and caste systems. "I don't expect them to know the content," she explained, "but how they respond gives me a heads-up about the distribution of knowledge in the room." Based on the results, Ms. Montgomery puts together online learning modules and sets up stations focused on different facets of the unit. "I give them the pre-assessment results so that they can see what their learning needs are, and they set goals accordingly," she said. "I run exploration periods each week so they can select the stations they need most." She also provides her students with short online quizzes so they can monitor their progress. "These aren't for grades. These are for goals," she explained. Digital badges are awarded for successful completion of modules and stations, and when students have earned all the assigned badges for the unit, they take the final assessment. "This means that some students are finished with the unit before others. That allows them time for exploration and enrichment, which includes peer tutoring."

Peer tutoring is one element she uses to support students with disabilities. Ms. Montgomery's middle school has long been inclusive, meaning that students with disabilities are enrolled in general education classes and have appropriate supports available. She works with special educator Angelo Matapang, who supports the entire grade-level team. "Mr. Matapang and I collaborate to figure out the accommodations some students with IEPs will need, such as adjusting reading materials and using dictation software to support writing," she said. Mr. Matapang added, "There are a few students in 6th grade with more significant disabilities. So I take on the modifications that are needed, such as using augmentative communication devices and consulting with the content teacher to figure out what the essential concepts are for the unit."

21. *Educators have access to professional learning that builds their technical and intellectual skills.*

There's always more to learn, and the way for us to be a better teacher next year than we are this year is to keep learning. But not all learning is equally effective or useful. We've all been to boring, useless, and ineffective professional development sessions that had no impact on our lives. We leave these sessions saying, "I will never get those two hours back." We have also had amazing learning experiences that have directly affected how we think about teaching and learning. The National School Boards Association (Coleman, Negrón, & Lipper, 2014) identified five essential factors for effective professional learning:

1. The duration of professional development efforts must be significant and ongoing to allow time for teachers to learn a new strategy and grapple with the implementation problem.
2. There must be support for a teacher during the implementation stage that addresses the specific challenges of changing classroom practice.
3. Teachers' initial exposure to a concept should not be passive but rather should engage teachers through varied approaches so they can participate actively in making sense of a new practice.
4. Modeling is highly effective in helping teachers understand a new practice.
5. The content presented to teachers shouldn't be generic but instead specific to the discipline (for middle school and high school teachers) or grade level (for elementary school teachers).

One of the ways that these five tenets can come alive in a school is through the implementation of collaborative planning teams as part of a larger professional learning community (DuFour, DuFour, Eaker, & Many, 2010). For example, the teachers at Silver Lake Elementary School collaborated with their peers to address four PLC questions:

1. What is it we want our students to learn?
2. How will we know if each student has learned it?
3. How will we respond when some students do not learn it?
4. How can we extend and enrich the learning for students who have demonstrated proficiency? (p. 119)

Using these four questions, the teachers talked about the standards and how to design units of study that would help students to master the standards. They also developed common assessments so that they would know which of their students had mastered the content and which still needed support. As part of their meetings, the PLC members examined student work and talked through ideas about actions they could take to ensure that all students learned. They also discussed interventions for students who had not yet mastered the content and how to extend the learning of those who had already mastered the content.

In addition to collaborative learning team discussions, professional learning can involve events in which information is shared with a group. These types of events are typically better for introductory information, motivational experiences, or learning how to implement a skill. We don't mean to discount these types of seminars, but if ideas are going to become action, ongoing support and coaching is necessary.

We are not going to dive too deeply into professional learning experiences other than to say that teachers deserve high-quality learning experiences just like their students do. Our point in raising the issue of professional learning in a book on equity is to ensure that all teachers have access to quality professional learning and that the time spent in professional learning sessions aligns with the data uncovered in equity audits. For example, when the teachers at Horace Mann High School noticed that there were few differentiation tools being used at their school, they decided to do something about that, believing that increased differentiation would address some of the equity gaps that had persisted. They realized that the majority of teachers did not have content-specific ideas for differentiation, so they searched for people who could share their experiences. They found a school in a neighboring district that had success with differentiation and invited teachers from different content areas to meet with Mann teachers in a workshop setting. As directed, the Mann teachers each brought an upcoming unit of study to the session. They were introduced to a wide range of techniques for differentiating, including these, courtesy of a history teacher from the neighboring school:

- **Compacting.** Pre-assessing students and aligning learning to the identified gaps.
- **Independent projects.** Inviting students to choose a project that demonstrated their individual understanding.
- **Tiered assignments.** Increasing choice in assignments such that students demonstrate understanding in different ways.
- **Flexible grouping.** Forming learning groups for collaboration that are different from those groups that met with the teacher.
- **Learning centers.** Setting up stations so that smaller groups of students are working on content collaboratively.

This same teacher also passed around student work samples demonstrating different approaches to differentiating content, process, and products. Following these introductory comments, she invited the teachers from Mann to identify opportunities for differentiation within the lessons they were about to teach. They worked collaboratively, in course-alike groups, thinking about ways that they could reach more of their students. They agreed to meet in two weeks to share student work samples to determine which tools were most effective and then share those with teachers throughout their school.

First Steps: It Starts with You

Invest in your own professional learning by embracing or deepening peer collaboration. If you currently plan alone, partner with a peer to meet each week for 30 minutes to discuss students or content you have in common. If you already plan regularly with peers, commit to engaging in collegial coaching with a colleague—which means visiting each other's classrooms and providing guiding questions for one another to prompt thinking. If you already observe and are routinely observed by peers, then engage in a round of microteaching. This involves video-recording your instruction, then meeting with a colleague to view and discuss what you are noticing about student learning. These investments in your own professional learning through peer collaboration will elevate your skill set.

Conclusion

Instructional excellence doesn't happen by decree. It must be carefully nurtured through ongoing professional learning that promotes the technical and intellectual development of teachers. This professional learning feeds the learning of students, who benefit from intentional instruction that communicates the purpose of learning and fosters the acquisition, consolidation, and extension of knowledge.

In terms of equity, all students must have access to high-quality instruction and some predictability in their learning experiences. In addition, all students need teachers to notice their needs and respond accordingly. Unfortunately, in some classrooms and schools, needs are identified but not addressed. In those cases, inequity is exacerbated, and membership in the classroom or school is questioned. We have seen our fair share of under-taught students who have been recommended for alternative placements.

One student who comes to mind was told by an administrator that the classes at his school were "too hard for him" and that "he would get better grades at an easier school." Rather than focus on the systems changes necessary to ensure that his learning needs (and the learning needs of all students) were met, this administrator focused her efforts on encouraging this student (and other struggling students) to transfer out. To our thinking, you have to be pretty embarrassed about your school and insecure about your ability to create change if you are actively trying to send students away.

We should all be proud of our instructional program. If it is not yet effective in ensuring that all students reach mastery, then it's time to identify areas of need and develop a plan to address them. The data are clear: when students have effective teachers, they learn a lot and can overcome significant gaps in their prior learning. But it's not as simple as saying that teachers matter. In order to make schools into more equitable learning environments, we must ensure all students experience effective instruction. Effective teachers know how to facilitate learning for everyone.

CHAPTER 5

Engaged and Inspired Learners

Students Taking Responsibility for Their Futures

Vontriece (she goes by V) is the kind of student teachers dream of, and we are lucky to know her. She is a spoken-word poet who composes open verse that makes your heart stop. She excels in all her academic classes and can be counted on to tutor fellow students who struggle with lessons. Out and proud, she is a driving force in our school's LGBTQ community. She interns at a hospital, and her preceptors there love her calm and mature presence with patients. Now an 11th grader, V is looking at a variety of public and private universities, where she will undoubtedly be seen as an asset on campus. She knows what her aspirations are and pursues them. She builds relationships with peers and adults who further expand her network, and she seeks out opportunities to enrich her experiences. V's also fortunate to go to a school where the conditions are right for her. In a different place, she might fit the profile of a bullied or ostracized student: her race, sexual identity, interests, and demeanor could make her a target elsewhere. We would argue that in a school where equity is front and center, V is benefiting from the social-emotional engagement, opportunity to learn, and instructional excellence that drive continuous improvement.

Mystique is a different story altogether. We came to know her last year as a combative, argumentative, and volatile 9th grader who enrolled at our school mostly so she could spend more time with her 10th grade girlfriend.

Riding the waves of adolescent romances can be difficult for any secondary educator; in this case, the tempest is compounded by Mystique's low self-esteem and diminished sense of agency. The only tool she seems to have is anger, and her prickly nature makes it difficult to get close to her. She's just the kind of student who might easily be written off as a lost cause. After all, it's much more rewarding to bask in the warm light V casts than to spend time with a grumpy, crying, angry Mystique.

And yet we're seeing small signs that she's making progress. Now in 10th grade, Mystique has told us she wants to be called "PM," as in "Positive Mystique." The conversations she's had with caring adults over the past year are helping her to realize that her gruff demeanor isolates her from her peers, who tend to back away from her after she rejects their early overtures. She's trying to repair and rebuild those relationships, and she is spending more sustained time in class. Admittedly, it is two steps forward, one step back with Mystique. There are still angry words and even physical confrontations. But another thing that's helping is a bracelet Dominique gave her with two beads on it. One bead contains a drop of water from Mount Everest, and the other bead has mud from the Dead Sea. Mystique wears it remind to herself to be humble when she reaches high points in her day and to stay hopeful when she's at the low point. That's her aspiration right now. She knows that mastering her emotions is going to be critical for her personal and academic success.

We profiled these two young women (both names are pseudonyms) to illustrate the range of children and adolescents educators work with every day. Some, like V, are model students, and they make us feel incredibly good about what we do. It is easy to stay connected with kids like this, and to be on the lookout for opportunities that align with their aspirations. Others are like Mystique, whose battles with the world and herself make it much more difficult for us to connect with her and support her. But we know that both girls, as all people do, exhibit communicative intent in their behaviors. V draws you in; you can't help but like her, and you want to do things that support her growth. Although Mystique's behaviors seem designed to push others away, what she's trying to communicate is that she wants to be heard and noticed. The voice and aspirations of students run on a broad continuum from nearly self-actualized to wandering in the desert. As educators, it is our duty to help every one of them gain knowledge of themselves, the world, and how they want to fit into it.

That's no simple task. So far, this book has focused on creating the conditions necessary for students to find their own voices and strive toward achieving their own aspirations. The entire Building Equity Taxonomy was designed to lead to this pinnacle moment. We submit that when educators change the structural conditions of schools to increase equity, they increase the likelihood that students will understand their potential, work to develop it, and go on to maximize it.

Consider this poem, written by Tosh, a 7th grader:

I aspire to:
Not give in to pressure
Join the Navy or Army (to pay for my college)
Go to college (preferably SDSU)
Attend a culinary institute
Become a homeowner
Live there with the one I love (and have a dog too)
Have someone write a book about my life (and maybe that book can be turned into a movie)
Maybe be an actor (I could play me in my story)
Play soccer (and maybe be a coach)
Be successful.

The middle school staff were surprised when Tosh's teacher read this poem aloud at our morning stand-up meeting. Everyone knew that Tosh had a challenging home life and that he often brought those challenges to school in the form of either checking out or acting out. At the time we write this, Tosh is yet to be a consistently engaged and inspired student; most of his needs are related to the social-emotional issues addressed in Chapter 2. However, Tosh's poem reminded us that all of the trauma in his life has yet to crush his ability to think about the future and aspire to something different. We mention Tosh as a reminder that although the Building Equity

Taxonomy presents a hierarchy of issues to attend to, work on them is not necessarily discrete or completely linear. Often we must approach them in a fluid and multidirectional manner.

The first four levels of the taxonomy are devoted to our responsibilities and opportunities as educators to cultivate the conditions that result in an engaged and inspired student body. The decisions we make to accept these responsibilities and seize these opportunities are about creating more structurally equitable schools. Think of it this way: making purposeful structural changes to create the conditions that foster inspiration are our inputs. To make these inputs, we might need to invest our brain power, financial resources, time, and skill resources differently. Through these inputs, we can change the conditions at the starting line where our students gather and change conditions during the race itself. Ultimately, though, what we all want to know is how does the race end—which means, in education terms, *what and how well do all students learn*, and *what do they do with their learning?* These are the outputs of equity work. The only way to truly evaluate the equity of our school practices is to examine the effect they have on *our entire student body*, not just the standouts, the valedictorians, the class president. Everything up to now in this book has been about educators' preparation and actions to create more equitable conditions. Just as everything in Maslow's hierarchy was designed to identify conditions associated with need fulfillment, the Building Equity Taxonomy was designed to help manipulate the inputs in order to maximize the outputs.

"I know who I am. I know where I am going. I have a plan. This school has helped me discover myself. This school is part of my plan for where I'm going." When Yasser, a 12th grader at our school, shared those words in an unplanned exchange with some visitors in the hallway, we looked at each other, knowing we had just heard something profound. This was the statement of an engaged and inspired student. This was confirmation that he was preparing to leave us with a sense of agency that would allow him to open doors of opportunity. It was something Yasser had developed over the years, as he moved from a 9th grader playing guitar for senior citizens in a long-term care facility, to 10th grader interning in a hospital pathology lab, to an

11th grader interning in an inpatient mental health facility, to a 12th grader who was completing six units of transferable psychology courses at the local community college and aspiring to be a biochemical neurologist. As school leaders, we aspire to create a student body in which each child can say what Yasser did: *I know who I am, I know where I am going, and school is a part of my plan to get there.* And we believe this is possible only when we provide an equitable school experience.

Why Engaged and Inspired Learners Are Important for Equity

Every school can point with pride to amazing students who take our breath away because of their kindness, academic prowess, leadership skills, or community activism. These students motivate us to do the hard work of school every day. But schools that produce only a handful of such young people have all the evidence they need that their school has inequitable systems. These are the outcome data that should trouble us deeply. Is the 9th grade class larger than the 12th grade class? Those kids didn't just disappear. Somehow systems failed them. Did 30 percent of the kindergartners miss 10 or more days of school? Multiply the lost instructional hours and wonder what might have occurred if they had been there with you. No school, including ours, can call itself truly equitable until every single student gets what he or she needs to strive and to grow.

Looking Forward by Looking Back

In Chapter 1, we reflected on the persistent inequities that are a legacy of segregated education and talked about how we educators must challenge ourselves and our communities by promoting better and more frequent physical integration. In Chapter 2, we argued that equity demands sensitivity to the mental health and well-being of our entire student body, and the promotion of practices that make our schools more welcoming, safer places for them and their families. In Chapter 3, we submitted that schools that educators work to make safe and welcoming will still be inequitable unless they also work to expand and support opportunities to learn for each student.

And then, in Chapter 4, we highlighted the power of quality instruction, noting that teachers do their best work when there are schoolwide agreements about excellent instructional practices and systems to support students who falter. Once again, all four of these conditions, reflected in the first four levels of the Building Equity Taxonomy, are mutually dependent conditions. For example, a teacher's effectiveness will be limited if the school does not have responsive systems for students' mental health needs. Opportunities to learn will be limited if resources are available within one department but not another. We will argue in this chapter that reaching the pinnacle of the Building Equity Taxonomy is dependent on adequately attending to each of the levels it rests on.

When educators look at their school's entire student body, especially in majority-minority schools, they want to be able to say that all students are capable and accomplished learners

- Who are continuously building and reinforcing their identity and agency.
- Who have been empowered to use and direct their education toward exploring and pursuing their interests, skills, and aspirations.
- Who complement their dreams with viable action plans and opportunities.

Almost all schools have some students who fit this bill—their Vs and Yassers. However, seeking equity means refusing to believe it's acceptable for even a small percentage of students to fall short of this goal—to feel lost, or voiceless, or defeated, or hopeless, or aimless. Staff at Del Rio Middle School were proud of the academic accomplishments of a large percentage of their student body, so they were shocked to find Building Equity Audit evidence that 64 percent of students felt unsafe and bullied at school. Alerted to this significant problem, they made a plan and took action. When Highlands Middle conducted the audit, only 18 percent of students reported feeling unsafe at school. Can we say, though, that safety and bullying is not a problem at Highlands? This school has 750 students, and 18 percent represents 135 students who feel unsafe at school. Is that "acceptable"? More important, what percentage of those 135 students will feel like V when they enter their junior year of high school, and what percentage will enter high school feeling like Mystique—too afraid or too angry to invest in their own empowerment and aspirations?

As we will discuss further in Chapter 6, completing equity audits of our schools and responding to the implications of the evidence becomes part of a continuous cycle of program improvement and refinement. This work is never done, and we must be cautious of accepting a good outcome when our goal is a great one. Schools that are building equity must become more proficient at fostering the great outcome of student empowerment. Here are a few points to keep in mind:

- Empowering students includes nurturing their leadership capacity and including their voices in decisions about the operation of the classroom and school.
- Student aspirations drive school goals and must be aligned to both current realities as well as future possibilities.
- Students' growth mindset must be nurtured. Educators do this by giving them practice setting personal best goals, monitoring their own progress, and developing resiliency to overcome social, emotional, and academic setbacks.
- Assessment-capable learners use knowledge of their current performance, compare that with the expected levels of performance, and seek feedback to achieve their aspirations.

We don't naively believe that every student will simultaneously reach these upper levels of empowerment. But laying out a path for all students, and then walking it with them, is essential to a journey of this magnitude.

Engaging and Inspiring Students Through Leadership and Decision Making

Engagement cannot exist without opportunities to decide. People whose lives are ruled by the decisions of others and have no forum to exercise their voices are marginalized, even silenced. It's ironic that traditional school organizations espouse democratic ideals but rarely allow students much voice in how their school operates. We're talking about more than student government here, or choices about the prom theme. Our concern is the voice students have, individually and in groups, to make important decisions about themselves and what they learn.

No, students are not adults, and we acknowledge that giving them license to decide everything is not in their best interests. But we blunt their development when we do not allow them some kind of decision-making role. How can young people possibly learn about themselves, the world, and their ability to positively affect both, if they are never a participant in the decisions that affect their learning?

Curricular leadership

Our ultimate goal as educators is the empowerment of students, defined as "ownership of learning" (Reeves, 2008, p. 84). We need students to be partners with us in the learning process. However, student decision making about curriculum makes some educators uncomfortable, especially as they confront the mechanisms necessary for such changes. Most educators are amenable to concepts related to growth mindset and resilience but may be less comfortable with getting feedback from students about their teaching, for instance. Some teachers are more agreeable to notions about offering choice in the curriculum but may be a bit more worried about having students making decisions about how much time should be devoted to a unit of study. (Wait, isn't it the teacher who decides when the unit is completed?) An inspired and engaged student body isn't something that can be accomplished through wishful thinking. It happens when we couple intentions with actions and policies.

Teachers often create choice within the curriculum to enhance learning and foster interest. However, the traditional approach is that the teacher creates a menu of possible assignments or projects, and the students then choose from the preselected list. This is really a forced choice, in the sense that the options are prescribed in advance, and students don't have the opportunity to opt out. True student choice involves student-teacher collaboration to generate the options.

As one example, Health Sciences High features four schoolwide essential questions each year, one per quarter. Essential questions (McTighe & Wiggins, 2013) are not easily answered; they are intended to encourage inquiry and debate, fueled by knowledge development in the classroom. Each spring, students, adults, and community members in our middle school and high school nominate possible questions for consideration. These appear on a digital ballot, but only students are eligible to vote. The top four become the schoolwide questions for the following year, ordered to align with the content being taught during the quarter. Examples from past years vary from the philosophical ("What is beautiful?") to the controversial ("What's worth fighting or even dying for?"). Occasionally, we're a bit mystified with our students' choices (e.g., "You exist, but do you live?"). More often, we are humbled by their depth of thinking (e.g., "Can money buy you happiness?" "Does gender matter?").

One essential question generated discussions and investigations that were particularly profound: "What is race and does it matter?" Needless to say, it's a challenge for us as adults to find ways to talk about a subject that makes most of us uncomfortable, but we owe it to our students to show them how we struggle to make sense of this enormous question. "Wow," exclaimed 11th grader Marcus, "you really are willing to keep it real!" It was as if we had passed some authenticity litmus test. Carmen Avery, who teaches English, shared her perspective on this essential question: "The students respect the fact that we are acknowledging something very important and relevant to them, to their identities, to their struggles. [Race] is what is bombarding them in the news and on the streets. This is what is on their minds. We are finally giving them permission to discuss the elephant in the room, and it's been there for a long time." The challenge is to find out what is really important—vitally important—to your students and then look for opportunities to allow them to explore those subjects in educationally sound ways. If we "keep it real," students are likely to "really engage."

We will use one more example from our middle school to explain what choice in curriculum means for student engagement and inspiration. For a few years now, health educator Shayna North has been beginning each semester by introducing the content she is required to teach, which includes sexual health, nutrition, physical fitness, and substance abuse. Then students vote on the number of weeks they would like to devote to each topic, understanding that while they can't vote content out all together, they can have a say in how much time is devoted to each topic. It's not surprising that these young adolescents want more time to understand how to take care of themselves and each other when it comes to sexual health. However, it doesn't occupy the entire curriculum. At the end of each week, the teacher surveys the students to gauge when it's time to move on.

Among the structures Ms. North has set up to ensure her students feel heard are class meetings and circles (see Chapter 2) to resolve classroom issues that impede learning, using them to bolster social-emotional engagement. She also capitalizes on student leadership and voice by creating a forum for her students to provide feedback to her. Face-to-face meetings can be a great way for teachers, especially those who work with younger children, to gather feedback about their teaching.

Teachers at Putnam Intermediate School, which serves grades 4–8, embrace this approach. In Derek Doan's 6th grade classroom, students complete a survey after each unit of study. Mr. Doan uses an online poll, and his students answer three quantitative questions on a scale of 1–4 (1 = needs improvement, 2 = average, 3 = good, 4 = excellent):

1. Rate how I [the teacher] gave useful feedback on your learning during this unit.
2. Rate how responsive I was to your learning needs.
3. Rate how clearly I communicated the purpose for learning and success criteria throughout this unit.

In addition, the students answer three open-ended questions:

1. Was this unit too hard or too easy for you? Why?

2. What should I be sure to keep when I teach this unit next year?

3. What advice do you have for me about how to improve?

Students at Putnam Intermediate are taught about the difference between constructive feedback and mean comments, but they are not required to put their names on the survey. "It's hard for anyone to look at criticism," said Mr. Doan. "But I have to admit it has really helped me. The kids are actually really respectful and thoughtful." After Mr. Doan distributes the results of the unit test to his students, he displays the feedback he received in the form of bar graphs and comment summaries. "The fact that I know I'm going to ask my students for feedback keeps me on my toes." The school doesn't have a single instrument; rather, it requires each teacher to develop and regularly administer a survey that is aligned with their professional goals. "Feedback and purpose were two areas of identified need that my principal and I came up with last year," Mr. Doan said. "That's why those items are on this year's survey. I tell them I need their help in becoming a stronger teacher each and every year." These student feedback results are a part of the evidence teachers submit for annual evaluations. "I revisit my goals with the administrator, and discuss with her how I'm using reflection and innovation to strengthen my teaching," said Mr. Doan. "It's changed the way I perceive my role in their lives."

Self-determination

"I want to be a veterinarian because I like animals." How often have you heard a statement like this from a student? If the child is small, say 6 or 7 years old, it might be greeted with a smile and a pat on the head. But when it's a 9th grader who has racked up 12 absences in the first 45 days of school, who doesn't complete his math homework because he's "dumb," and who "hates science," it's quite worrying. This is a common dilemma for educators and counselors who want to be sensitive to the desires of students and don't want to trample on anyone's dreams. But when nothing in a student's history suggests he is equipped to achieve the dream he shares, it's hard to respond with anything but a sympathetic look and a mumbled, "That's a good goal."

Self-determination is achieved through informed decision making. Therefore, students must have accurate information about themselves in order to align their decision making with their aspirations. They need the tools to develop goals and gauge their progress toward them. This is because student aspirations are complex, filtered through several constructs (Eccles, 2009), including

- **Self-concept.** How does your school ability compare to that of others?
- **Value.** How interesting is the content to you? Are you studying hard to do well?
- **Educational aspirations.** What level of postsecondary education do you plan to attain?
- **Occupational aspirations.** What sort of work do you think you'll do for a living?

Unfortunately, occupational aspirations seem to consume most of the conversation between children and adults, beginning with "What do you want to be when you grow up?" But it is rare for the adult to follow with discussions of the student's self-concept, values, and educational aspirations in relation to an occupational aspirations. The would-be veterinarian we mentioned, Santiago, needed several interventions to get on track. His absences were of immediate concern, and further work with the family revealed that limited access to health care—a common dilemma in the impoverished, rural community where he lived—was a major factor keeping him out of class. The school reached out to community resources in order to make health care more accessible to him and to a number of other students in the school facing similar circumstances.

In time, Santiago's improved attendance helped him see for the first time that he wasn't dumb, as he had feared, but rather that missing so much school meant he was always playing catch-up. His school made sure he enrolled in career pathway courses that included animal science, agricultural biology, and veterinary science. For the first time in his academic career, he understood that the prerequisites to admittance into a veterinary program included successful completion of Algebra 1 and Biology. This shift in his planning helped him understand the value of the high school courses he was taking and why he needed to complete them. The student had opportunities to explore occupational paths and learned that there were a number of different options available to him. When the student realized that being a veterinarian required a doctoral degree, he announced that he didn't want to go to school for so many years. But his fieldwork with a local large-animal veterinarian helped him decide that he did want to become a veterinary nurse, which required an associate degree. To fund his college education, Santiago decided to work after high school graduation as a veterinary assistant for the same doctor where he had done his fieldwork. In three years, he had earned his associate's degree in the field of his choice.

Schools typically do a huge disservice to students who don't have a plan for how to achieve their aspirations. In middle and high school, this becomes a critical issue, but aspirations can and should be encouraged and nurtured much sooner. Dominique's son Nixon, who is in elementary school, is an example. On Nixon's first day of kindergarten a few years ago, each child was asked to pose with a sign that included the school name and date, the child's name, and a sentence that said, "I want to be a _____ when I grow up." (Nixon's answer: a police officer.) Cute, right? But it was more than a darling photograph of a little boy with big dreams. It provided Nixon's teacher with information about what interested her young student, and she made sure the classroom library featured stories like *Officer Buckle and Gloria* (Rathmann, 1995). Nixon's extended family gained another way of talking with him about his interest in public safety, and they helped him strike up conversations with school crossing guards and off-duty police officers working at public events.

The counselor at this elementary school employs the three-part National Model framework for student competencies: academic, career, and social-emotional development (American School Counselor Association, 2017). As such, the counselor provides structured lessons on workers at school and in the community, and links them to classroom jobs the children have. For example, one lesson focused on why it is important for students to be honest when doing their classroom jobs, and to complete the job on time. Dominique's son, who loves it when it's his turn to be the line leader, commented, "If I'm late and it's my turn, everyone else misses recess time." Early lessons on classroom jobs should bring in opportunities to talk about work habits and ethics of school success, and link them to the same values that are needed in any job. Although young children will of course shift their aspirations (after attending a summer zoo program, Nixon now wants to be a scientist), these fundamental concepts exist in all careers.

Goal setting

Inspired by the work of Boston Philharmonic Orchestra conductor Benjamin Zander and his wife Rosamund (2000), mathematics teacher Andrea Halstead gave all of her statistics students an *A* for the class on the first day. All she requested in return was each student write and send her a letter dated the last day of class and describing why they earned the *A*. She reviews these letters and then holds each student to the expectations they had for themselves as an *A* student.

We want our students to be intrinsically motivated to learn rather than rely on external motivators such as grades, points, stickers, and other rewards. We want them to construct a personal narrative of themselves as successful students. We want their narrative to fuel their own growth mindset. We want them to visualize success, and give voice to it, and then to act accordingly. Isn't that what empowerment is? However, the fact is that we all are motivated by, and accountable to, a combination of internal and external factors. By way of illustration, we are writing this book because we are intrinsically motivated to commit our thoughts to the page, but we're also extrinsically motivated by timelines to deliver this manuscript. Unfortunately, grades are too often misused as an extrinsic tool to control (reward/ punishment) instead of used wisely to inform students (feedback) about their learning (Guskey, 2014). Using grades to control students can negatively influence the kinds of goals students set for themselves and diminish the value of goal setting.

Many elementary and secondary classrooms use goal setting as a means to positively influence learning, as goals are linked to the actions that students take (Morisano & Locke, 2013). But they need to be the right kind of goals if they are going to positively influence learning. There are two categories: *mastery goals* and *performance goals*.

Mastery goals are the more desirable of the two, because these are the ones that focus attention on gaining knowledge and expertise. Mastery goals are about the learning ("I want to become fluent in Spanish"), while performance goals are about the outcome ("I want to get an *A* in my Spanish class"). Although it might not seem on the surface to be a big deal, over time, emphasis on performance goals undermines learning, as the student's focus is on avoiding looking incompetent in the eyes of others, avoiding mistakes, and avoiding risk-taking because of a fear of failure (Morisano & Locke, 2013). A student who intentionally fails a math placement test in order to be assigned to an easier course of study has performance goals, not mastery goals, in mind. On the other hand, mastery goals position students where you want them to be. When the goal is to become more fluent in Spanish, the teacher is now a resource rather than a judge, collaboration with peers becomes a way to learn, and errors are understood as being a part of the learning process, rather than something to be avoided at all costs.

Mastery goals are directly related to one's sense of competence in learning. A shift to a competency grading system that allows students to retake tests they passed, but are not satisfied with, further reinforces a mastery goal mindset. Megan McCrary, a 9th grade English teacher at the school where we work, fosters a mastery goal mindset with her students. She recalled a time when, prior to teaching a unit on nonlinear plot structures in fiction, she administered a pre-assessment so that students would see their present level of knowledge. The average pre-assessment score for the grade level was a zero—not surprising. But after the unit, the average score was 84.3 percent, a solid *B* average. The students were proud of their accomplishments, but Ms. McCrary challenged them toward mastery, even in her feedback. "My feedback is always structured to support a growth mindset," she said. "For example, if a student earns less than full credit on any short-answer question [I might ask], 'What more can you say to demonstrate your understanding or mastery of the content?' If a student has answered any short-answer question earning full credit beyond simply meeting expectations [I might say], 'Your answer is very thorough, and I can tell that you put a lot of effort into it. Great work!'"

Because students can retake competencies to improve passing grades, Ms. McCrary gets lots of takers. For this particular assessment, nearly half (46 percent) of her 155 students chose another attempt. Among the retakers, the average score grew to 94.3 percent, a full 10 percentage points higher. "Students retaking the post-assessment clearly read and *applied* my initial feedback," Ms. McCrary said. "Sharing and celebrating this will create a ripple effect."

A growth mindset

Aspirations and goal setting are nested into a growth mindset. Students with a growth mindset believe that intelligence is a function of learning and can be acted upon ("understanding photosynthesis is hard, but by reading and studying about it, I can learn it"), while those with a fixed mindset believe that intelligence is static ("I'm not smart enough in science"). These principles, described by Carol Dweck in a series of influential publications (see Dweck, 2007), have changed how we talk about our students. But the author herself expresses misgivings about how growth mindset is misapplied as it relates to effort. Here are some comments she published in *Education Week*:

> Recently, someone asked what keeps me up at night. It's the fear that the mindset concepts, which grew up to *counter* the failed self-esteem movement, will be used to *perpetuate* that movement. In other words, if you want to make students feel good, even if they're not learning, just praise their effort! Want to hide learning gaps from them? Just tell them, "Everyone is smart!" The growth mindset was intended to help close achievement gaps, not hide them. It is about telling the truth about a student's current achievement and then, together, doing something about it, helping him or her become smarter. (Dweck, 2015, p. 20, emphasis original)

In other words, mindset is an equity issue. If our fumbled attempts to foster a growth mindset lead us to praise effort without providing informative feedback or teaching students strategies for recovery, then we contribute to inequitable systems. However, when we work with intentionality by ensuring that every student has aspirations, a plan to get there, and a growth mindset to draw upon, we foster self-determination.

Engaged and Inspired Students Are Assessment-Capable Decision Makers

Academic goals fueled by a growth mindset require that students are aware of where they are, and where they want to be, in order for them to monitor their progress and make adjustments. These students understand their current level of performance and use information (such as assessments and teacher feedback) to make decisions about learning opportunities that will build their skill sets. Hattie (2012) calls these students "assessment-capable learners." These are students who can answer these three questions about their learning (Hattie & Timperley, 2007):

- *Where am I going?* What is it I want to learn?
- *How am I going?* Where am I right now, and how can I bridge the gap?
- *Where to next?* What is the plan to get to my learning destination?

But without teachers' willingness to be transparent with students about their learning, students remain reliant on teachers to tell them when they have learned and when they have not. They are left viewing school as a place where other people make the rules, tell you what to do and when to do it, and judge you for your efforts. Is it any wonder so many students disconnect from educators? Has our hesitancy to let students make decisions about their own learning prevented us from using the best tools at our disposal—students knowing and owning their learning progress?

Much has been written about the use of assessment for learning and its link to quality instruction. We want to highlight an interesting finding noted in a systematic review of 117 studies on assessment for learning (AfL), specifically looking at factors that enhanced or constrained student learning (Heitink, Van der Klejj, Veldkamp, Schildkamp, & Kippers, 2016). The researchers noted that in situations where students were not meaningfully involved in formative assessment, student progress was hindered. Examples of meaningful student involvement included immediate and actionable feedback, less emphasis on grades and scores compared to learning, and peer- and self-assessments. It's interesting that teacher beliefs also were an important factor:

> [T]he quality of AfL practices is influenced by the extent to which teachers feel responsible for student attainment of goals rather than just coverage of the curriculum. Teachers with less of a feeling of responsibility also felt less inclination to evaluate student work, give effective feedback and revise teaching plans where needed. (Heitink et al., 2016, p. 56)

From the time children enter school, they need to be drenched in experiences that demonstrate their teachers' belief in them as being assessment-capable decision makers. Beginning in kindergarten, young children can self-assess their progress by comparing their advancement toward a class or individual goal. Using "I can" statements can help students see the purpose of the learning, as discussed in Chapter 4 and also help them determine their progress toward it. By early elementary, students should have regular experiences with peer assessments as they examine each other's work and provide feedback. This is not peer editing of each other's work, as the quality of the edits is limited by the knowledge of the novice editor. Rather, we ask students to provide responses to one another by reflecting back their understanding of the peer's work.

We have adopted the practice of text playback, described by Simmons (2003) as restating or retelling what the student understood after listening to or reading a classmate's writing. For instance, 7th graders Mark and Jacob exchanged drafts of their responses to their reading of *The Crossover* (Alexander, 2014). After Mark read Jacob's reading journal entry on the class discussion board, Mark wrote, "The most important idea you are sharing is that the fight on the basketball court that Josh and JB almost have is symbolism for their dad's heart problems. Josh calls their dad the 'backboard' of the family. You said that breaking the backboard in basketball is like breaking the rules of the game."

Several minutes later, after Jacob had read Mark's peer response, he replied, "I want to add that one brother seriously hurting another brother breaks a major rule in a family. You all stick together no matter what. I'm going to add that to my response so it's clear. Thanks."

Students who are assessment-capable understand that assessments are as much for their use as they are for their teachers. We saw this in evidence when seniors in our school who had enrolled in the community college trigonometry course were faced with an assessment on the first day of class. The students did not know this professor, but they got what she was looking for. They understood this was a pre-assessment that would inform the professor about what they already knew and inform themselves about their present level of knowledge. They took the online assessment and nobody freaked out about it. As each student got his or her results, they made comments like, "I didn't do well on this part. I forgot some of this from when I first learned it in summer school. Well, I guess I didn't really learn it yet." Another said, "This really helps me, because now I know where to put my efforts."

It's important to clarify that these 47 students (a third of the senior class) collectively fit every profile you have encountered in this book. Most live in poverty and belong to racial, ethnic, language, gender, or ability groups that might have been marginalized elsewhere. Quite a few of them have had serious difficulties with relationships with adults and peers, and nearly all have found themselves on one side or the other of a restorative practices table.

But they have also benefited from being in a school community that continues to critically examine the role of equity in the opportunities to learn and the structural access necessary to ensure their full participation. There are compensatory and adaptive practices in place to ensure that they succeed in rigorous coursework. We hope they are learning beside us as we leverage human and social capital by expanding their experiences, networks, and aspirations. College trigonometry is tough for high school seniors, without question. But the efforts schools engage in as they become increasingly culturally proficient and are oriented by a commitment to inspiring students should equip them with the tools they need to succeed.

Resilient Students Are Engaged Decision Makers

Resiliency is the ability to recover from setbacks. These setbacks are not narrowly quantifiable; they are perceptual. Some traumas are readily understood: being a victim of physical or emotional violence, suffering the loss of a loved one through death or separation, or experiencing a serious health crisis. Other stressors are less readily seen but may exist at moderate levels for protracted periods: difficulty at school, conflict with friends, romantic relationships, worries about the future, and family tensions, to name a few. But for children and adolescents living in poverty, these major traumas and moderate stressors are further complicated by unemployment in the family, or food insecurity, or homelessness, as well as the day-to-day grind of being poor. Looking closely at the lives of the students and families you serve can take your breath away. We are continually reminded of the path some of our students must walk each day just to get themselves to school on time: everything from taking responsibilities for helping with younger siblings and dealing with public transportation delays to coping with the lack of outerwear to keep themselves dry on a cold and rainy morning. We are in awe of students who persevere under these circumstances.

One's relative ability to bounce back from adverse occurrences is in part a function of personality, as responses to similar circumstances may cause one child to become angry, while a second shuts down, and a third takes action. Resilient people possess an optimistic view of the future, which should not be confused with happiness. There is a misconception that a child who is resilient is a happy child. However, a resilient child possesses a more positive self-concept and a stronger sense of agency than less resilient children (Garmezy, Masten, & Tellegen, 1984).

Teaching coping skills is vital for all students. Previous discussions about social-emotional learning and restorative practices once again figure into this aspect of student empowerment. Schools do much to foster the resiliency of students, and it should be noted that "[m]ost people make it despite exposure to severe risk. Close to 70 percent of youth from high-risk environments overcome adversity and achieve good outcomes" (Truebridge & Benard,

2013, p. 67). However, as an equity issue, it is vital that schools teach about resiliency, and the role of decision making, with intentionality. Henderson (2013) calls schools that have committed to do just that "safe haven schools." The safe haven school model's "Resiliency Wheel" (see Figure 5.1) encapsulates many of the principles we have elaborated on throughout the book. Opportunities to learn, social-emotional learning, high expectations, and caring and support are identified as protective factors for students.

FIGURE 5.1
The Resiliency Wheel

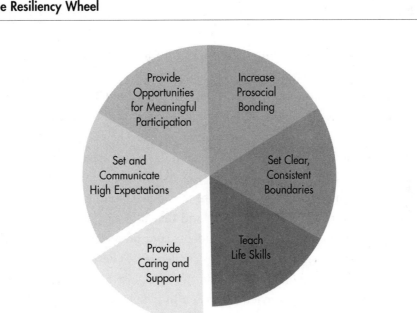

Source: From "Havens of Resilience," by N. Henderson, 2013, *Educational Leadership, 71*(1), p. 24. Copyright 2013 by ASCD.

Schools that actively foster resiliency make sure that children are surrounded by literatures that tell stories of overcoming adversity. These include biographies and autobiographies of famous figures, and—perhaps even more important—they show what it looks like to face challenges in everyday life. Cristina Garcia-Perez actively looks for these challenges in the books she reads to her transitional kindergarten (TK) students. Early in the school year, she introduces her students to *Don't Let the Pigeon Drive the Bus!* (Willems, 2003), a favorite of hers for talking about persistence. "The pigeon just won't give up, even though the bus driver keeps telling him no," Ms. Garcia-Perez chuckled. "But it's more than that. I want them to see that their typical 5-year-old behavior is a gift and a strength. I want my kids to stick with something when it means a lot to them." In discussions about the book, the teacher and her students talk about the pigeon's dream and all the different ways he tries to make it come true.

In a 3rd grade classroom at the same school, Jose Enriquez's students were discussing the dilemma that Bilal, a Muslim character, faces in *My Name Is Bilal* (Mobin-Uddin, 2005) when boys at his new school pull the hijab off of his sister's head. "My students need to see how other children face these problems, and what they do to resolve them," said the teacher.

For a time, Bilal wrestles with hiding his religious identity, and considers calling himself "Bill" to disguise his cultural origin. The children in the literature circle made a graphic organizer outlining the character's challenges and the coping skills he uses. "One of his coping skills was that he told a teacher, who helped him," said Roberto. "Write that down," said Cecilia. "And Bilal uses sports to get the bully to understand that he's a person with feelings." Later, Mr. Enriquez talked with his students about the ways the characters in this and other stories are able to meet challenges. "These are decisions that are made by these characters," he said. "It's not just being reactive. I want them to see that they can make a decision to talk with a trusted adult about their problems. They don't need to carry everything inside of them. That's making good decisions about oneself."

Engaged and Inspired Students Have a Human Rights Mindset

So what's our output? What kind of student do we want to send out into the world? A century ago, the answer was that we wanted a worker—someone who could perpetuate an existing society. Educators, therefore, were tasked with preparing students to assume their place in a class system that was governed by rules associated with wealth, race, ethnicity, and gender. Two world wars, a Soviet satellite launch, a civil rights movement, and a race to the Moon contributed to a shift in society's expectations of education.

As educators we began to look a bit harder at ourselves. We began to speak about "all students" even if our policies didn't always have their best interests in mind. By late in the 20th century, we saw the repercussions of failed policies that resegregated the schools we fought so hard to desegregate. We watched as the achievement gap, which had narrowed by the late 1980s, begin to widen again with each passing year. In a new century marked by international and domestic terrorism, growing economic disparities, fractured relationships between law enforcement and communities, and divisive public rhetoric that inflames everyone, we as educators are once again faced with the task of redefining ourselves for the good of our children.

We need to produce a generation of young people who care deeply about human rights, writ large and small. We need a generation that actively seeks out knowledge about the mistreatment of others and says, "I can do something about that." We need a generation that believes in the transformative power of advocating for others and uses its voice to resolve inequities that constrain human potential. But that won't ever happen if we don't do the same for them *now*. Today's youth will remember how their elders cared for them (or didn't care for them). How will they treat us when it is our turn to need them to advocate for us?

We must make sure—to the very best of our collective ability—that we do right by them. It begins with setting the conditions: integration, social-emotional engagement, opportunity to learn, and instructional excellence. But the output rests on the measure of the people we produce. Only by empowering students as decision makers do we set them on the path to make a positive difference locally and globally.

Earlier we told you that our current schoolwide essential question is about race. It's not easy to talk to students about the subject, especially when your racial identity doesn't match theirs. But no one said that school is easy, and the conversations and insights we have been privileged to be a part of are among the most rewarding of our careers. During this quarter, a black man in our community was killed in a confrontation with police officers. Like so many others in a distressing and unrelentingly long list of incidents like this one, his death has provoked protests and heated debate. We are hopeful that our school has become a place for adolescents to wrestle with such a difficult and painful topic in the company of people who care deeply for them. One young man, who identifies as African and Muslim, wrote this in his English class a few days after the shooting took place:

> ***Sirens***
> *Oh god please just let it be a speeding ticket*
> *Officer I'm sorry I know I passed the speeding limit*
> *I got my license and registration just wait a minute*
> *"Hands in the air" is all he shouts*
> *Bare hands up and he still takes shots*
> *Six in the chest for being born black*
> *My death caused by something I can't take back*
> *Your duty is to serve and protect*
> *Just 'cause I'm colored does that make me a suspect?*
> *Racist laws in effect*
> *While you guess it's easy to predict*
> *I'm next on the cops' most wanted list*
> *Before it was slashes/burns to show us our place*
> *Now it's a shell to remind us where we stay*
> *You can see the despair in our face*
> *With none to help to this day*
> *Daily prayers trying to reach dawn*
> *Help isn't a favor so why do you expect us to stay calm?*
> *Racism never ended, it's just being publicly displayed*
> *They wear blue*
> *Don't let them tell u that they're better than you*
> *Videos that have been recorded to show u what's true*
> *But it was brushed off their shoulders like it was nothing new*

They say not all cops are bad… don't blame us for a few
But the head is, and he controls the whole crew
But we're at fault when we use our rights to bear arms and flex it
'Cause know imma protect myself before I'm turned to a hashtag
So if we don't step up know what's gonna happen when our kids hear that
same siren
When they're also shot while grabbing their license
Know the world is not gonna change due to your silence
I'm not saying black lives matter more
I'm just saying they just matter too
And we're not here settling scores
We're just trying to stop this long living war so when our kids step out our
door we don't have to turn them into hashtags like the ones that came
before
So this is to remind you I'm not yours
Grasses at the grave greener 'cause of the black mom's tears
When u have ur kids is that what u want them to fear?
See this message couldn't get any more clear
My voice alone they will not hear
All lives matter is what they say
But the question is why are our lives the only ones being taken away…

We're moved by the despair in his words but heartened by the hope embedded within them. *Know the world is not gonna change due to your silence,* he writes. Here's a young man standing on the cusp of adulthood who understands a fundamental truth—that he matters, and that transformational change begins with him. *My voice alone they will not hear.* Yet he knows that one voice can be the start of something larger. His actions begin by using his words to touch the hearts and minds of others.

Caring communities are built with intention and with an eye on the needs of today's inhabitants as well as tomorrow's. A social justice mindset is necessary to build this caring community, and it is modeled through the actions and dispositions of the adults who surround young people. *Their* actions and dispositions are the output, and it is how we will be judged. How will the verdict read? What will our legacy be?

Building Equity Review Statements: Engaged and Inspired Learners

This chapter has focused on student voice and aspirations. When equity truly exists within a school, students are empowered to make decisions about their lives, their learning, and the issues that affect them. Schools with significant equity-focused staff know their students well and help students realize their aspirations—and not just their career aspirations. These students succeed in far greater numbers than students who do not believe that their efforts will yield any positive results.

Here are some key statements focused on gathering data to inform actions to address student empowerment.

22. Students are engaged in a wide range of leadership activities within the school.

In most schools, there are some students who are involved in leadership roles and the majority who are not. The typical way that schools provide leadership opportunities are student government and clubs. There is nothing wrong with these activities, and they do provide some students with opportunities to exercise their critical thinking and decision-making skills. Everyone can't be a part of student government, and we're not suggesting that they should. Instead, we think that educators have to figure out ways to provide students with a *range* of options to exercise their leadership.

We have been fortunate to observe a number of very different schools that have figured this out. For example, Brookhurst Elementary School provides students with classroom jobs. Students are elected monthly for these jobs, and the teachers have worked to develop descriptions for each role. Figure 5.2 contains a list of jobs for students in the primary and upper-elementary grades.

At the high school level, especially in schools that are large, educators must find ways to ensure that each student has a leadership opportunity. If they do not, students are likely to seek these opportunities elsewhere. We are reminded of Pedro, a 9th grader who had been expelled from several schools for stealing and selling stolen property. He was a difficult young man who required a lot of focused attention. He was gang-affiliated by the time we met him. After knowing him for a few years, we asked why he wanted to be part of a gang, and his response was, "You make your own decisions and face the consequences when you're in." Pedro wanted a leadership role, but his school had not been able to find one that worked for him.

FIGURE 5.2.
Classroom Jobs

Kindergarten–3rd Grade
- Attendance Assistant
- Paper Passer
- Line Leader
- Line Monitor
- Calendar Helper
- Number of the Day Helper
- Classroom Librarian
- Class Messenger
- Door/Light Monitor
- Recycling Chief
- Equipment Manager (Recess)
- Supply Manager (Classroom)
- Plant Caretaker
- Nurse Buddy
- Desk Checker
- Flag Salute Leader
- Computer Manager
- Lunch Helper

4th–6th Grade
- Attendance Assistant
- Paper Passer
- Class Messenger
- Pencil Sharpener
- Recycling Chief
- Equipment Manager (Recess)
- Supply Manager (Classroom)
- Homework Checker
- Plant Caretaker
- Desk Checker
- Flag Salute Leader
- Computer Manager
- Lunch Helper
- Time Manager (Schedules and Timers)
- Phone Operator
- Board Cleaner
- Teacher's Assistant

One of the many leadership roles Pedro took on during high school involved him participating in teacher interviews. He was part of a panel of students who met with each job candidate and then provided notes from these interactions to school leadership, who factored student feedback into the hiring decision. Pedro was very proud of this role and talked with other students about what questions he should ask. He talked with teachers about what they thought it meant to be a great teacher. Pedro took this role seriously.

During a series of interviews for a math teacher, Pedro asked each candidate what they would do if a fight broke out in their classroom. Most of the candidates provided standard, reasonable responses, such as ensuring safety, getting help, and reestablishing the learning environment. But one candidate stood out to Pedro. She said, "I would hope that a fight would never break out in my classroom because I have such strong relationships with students." After that, she provided additional information about getting help and so on. Pedro and the other students on the panel gave this candidate their highest recommendation. As it turned out, their comments were the deciding factor, and school leadership offered her the position.

Pedro removed himself carefully and slowly from the local gang, and was philosophical when members of his former gang beat him up. "I guess that's the price you pay for wanting power and control before you earned it," he said. Pedro ended up attending barber school as part of his senior year. He completed his training the summer after graduating and currently works full-time in a barber shop. He comes back to our school for every parents night, offering free haircuts for dads who come with their children. Knowing Pedro as we do, we believe that what he wanted all along was to be seen as a leader and have a little influence over his world.

Of course, not every high school student can serve on the teacher interview committee. There have to be lots and lots of leadership options available. At Mill River High School, the staff has a master list of students organized by grade level. Every quarter, they review their list, which is printed on poster paper. Next to each student's name is a box in which small dots can be placed. If the student is involved in sports, a yellow dot is added. If the student is involved in drama or music, a blue dot is added. For each such opportunity, there is a dot. And on that dot, written in pencil, is a letter: *P* for participating, *A* for actively engaged, and *L* for leading. The staff monitors the students in their school to see who is not involved in any type of connected activity and if leaders are emerging in this group. As the football coach noted,

"Yeah, I have the captain, but there are a lot of leadership opportunities on our team. I look for the qualities of a leader rather than the position. I want every athlete to feel part of the team, and that they have a say in how we operate as a team. That builds character, especially leadership character."

23. *Student aspirations are fostered.*

"Who do you want to be? What do you want to be? There's a difference, right? Let's focus on who you want to be and how your actions were or were not consistent," said school social worker Megan Hart. The middle school student she was meeting with had been in a fight, but he had calmed down enough to talk with her about what had happened.

Ms. Hart knew that she needed to connect Miguel's behavior with his aspirations if she had any hope in altering the course of action he'd take the next time someone pushed his buttons. She also knew that an inability to change could result in progressively stronger consequences, including eventual recommendations that he be removed from the school. Thankfully, Ms. Hart understands the power of fostering student aspirations. She knows that students who have a commitment to reaching their dreams behave in ways that are more consistent with those dreams. She also understands the reverse: students who do not have, or who are not able to articulate, aspirations are at high risk for acting out, school failure, and leading less satisfying lives after school.

When she asked Miguel who he wanted to be, he replied, "I want to be successful and have a lot of friends. I want people to say nice things about me, like they do about my dad. I want to be the kind of person who people respect, not because I can fight but because of who I am."

Ms. Hart responded, "I appreciate you sharing your aspirations. I haven't met your dad, but I'd like to, especially since people say positive things about him. What actions do you think make people say those kinds of things about him? What does he do specifically?"

Ms. Hart used her knowledge of aspirations to help Miguel rethink his actions, knowing that he would be less likely to act out this way after learning to connect goals for himself with what he chooses to do. Their conversation continued for nearly 20 minutes before Miguel said, "Today, I let someone else push me into doing something stupid. Can we call my dad and let him know what happened? And I will tell him what I learned from it."

We don't condone fighting as a learning opportunity, and we recognize that there are other actions that a school must take when students fight. But as we noted in an earlier chapter, students don't learn much from being suspended or expelled. They learn when they are required to make amends to the people they hurt. And they learn when they focus sharply on their aspirations, reflecting on the coherence of their dreams and actions.

Aspirations work is not limited to student behavior. Nor is it limited to students in middle or high school. Earlier in this chapter, we discussed Nixon's aspirations of becoming a police officer. Understanding who he wanted to become, his teacher provided him with a range of experiences that were linked with what he said. She did this with all of the students in her kindergarten class. As she said, "People sometimes say, 'They're only 5, and they really don't know what they want to be,' which is probably true for the vast majority of them. That doesn't mean that their aspirations should be ignored. That doesn't mean that their aspirations aren't real for them right now, or that their aspirations are fixed. I know that they'll change, but using what they tell me motivates them, provides me with natural connections, and helps them try on different personas as they grow and develop."

In addition to the natural connections teachers can make between learners and content when they know their students' aspirations, they can use this information to ensure that students complete a rigorous course of study. For years, Amira's career aspirations were to become a nurse, specifically an ICU nurse. Her school organized an internship experience and steered her toward a series of courses—Medical Biology, U.S. History and Public Health, and Advanced English and Public Health—that allowed her to see the connections between typical content and her vocational aspirations.

24. *Students select learning opportunities related to their interests.*

Engaged students make choices about their learning. They know what they want to know and be able to do, and they recognize their strengths and weaknesses. They select things to learn that match with their interests because they understand their vision for their future—at least to the degree associated with their developmental age. We're not suggesting that students simply be allowed to pick their own curriculum and learn only what they most want to learn; we don't think that a 2nd grader who loves dinosaurs should only learn about dinosaurs. What we're saying is that students should have opportunities to align the learning experiences that have been carefully designed to support mastery of required content standards with their interests. As a fairly simplistic example, a dinosaur-obsessed 2nd grader should be able to find plenty of time during independent reading and writing time to expand and refine her knowledge of dinosaurs. And resources that will allow her to do that should be available.

Consider the students in Melody Brooks's kindergarten class. As young as they are, every student knows where they are on the class's writing continuum. They can even explain their writing skills and where they need to grow. For example, Sasha said, "I am at a 5 right now. I want to get to a 6 by November and maybe a 10 for 1st grade. I leave spaces between words, but they don't always spell right. I get the first letter right most of the time but not all of the other letters. So I am working on writing the right words and using the word wall. I like writing when people read it." It's clear from Sasha's comments that she is interested in writing. She understands her current performance and what needs to happen for her to move forward. Her teacher supports this by encouraging Sasha to write about things that matter to her as she develops her skills. The work Ms. Brooks has done to explain the writing continuum and explain to students what they need to do to travel along it is empowering for all—and especially for those whose interests lie in this area.

Of course, there are other ways to guide student exploration of learning opportunities. The more than 700 students who attend Hawthorn Middle School, 90 percent of whom live in poverty, are provided time every Tuesday to work on their genius hour projects. These projects are self-selected and self-directed; students identify areas of inquiry and pursue them, developing proposals and timelines for their teachers to review and approve. For genius hour, Hawthorn divides the entire student body into mixed grade-level groups overseen by an assigned teacher, and students stay with the same teacher for all three years. During this time, they can extend their literacy, mathematics, science, social studies, interpersonal, artistic, or communication skills. Danny provided a glimpse into the experience from a student's perspective:

> Right now, I'm working on learning everything about cars because some day, I hope to make the next kind of car. I know that they are electric now, that's the current one. But did you know that they had steam cars? And then the kind that most people have now that have gas. I have learned about a lot of people who invented different cars and a lot about how cars work. My plans are to read about this every time I have genius hour and keep my notes on Google Docs. I scheduled a check-in presentation in two weeks, so I have to put my notes together. I'm going to make a video for part of my presentation and have some car parts to show people who are interested. I hope a lot of people pick my presentation because cars are really interesting and there can be a new one in the future.

Another way that students become engaged and inspired as they move from grade to grade is in the actual process of course selection. In many schools, students are assigned a standard course of study by grade level. In some high schools, students choose courses based on a career path that they have selected. In San Diego, where we are, there are schools that focus on technology, law enforcement, fine arts, business, culinary arts, health care, performing arts, and a host of other professions. In these career academies, content-area classes are taught through the lens of the particular career pathway. Students still learn algebra, for example, but the tasks they complete are aligned with their school's career pathway.

At Health Sciences High, we take this one step further. Within the lens of health care, students select their course of study in the upper division (grades 11 and 12). For example, they are offered options each semester, much like college students are. In the area of science, students can select chemistry, genetics, physics, environmental science, or sustainability. They can take medical Spanish, American Sign Language, psychology, public speaking, and a host of other courses. For students to make informed choices, they need to understand their aspirations and how these choices align with their goals.

25. *Students are provided authentic and applied learning experiences that link with their goals and aspirations.*

There are a number of ways to provide students with authentic and applied learning experiences such as field studies, internships, and citizenship development. Some people call these "real world" experiences, but we don't use that term; we believe that school is part of the real world, and we don't like to disparage the value of education. Having said that, our students can and do take advantage of these types of opportunities to engage in learning outside of the classroom and to better understand themselves as learners.

Take field studies, which are a critical part of the learning our students do within and beyond the classroom. In general, well-designed field studies require that teachers design a series of lessons to prepare students for the off-campus experience, followed by another series of in-class lessons that apply the learning gained through off-campus work. Contrast this with the typical field trip, which is often disconnected from the learning inside of school and of questionable educational benefit. Gone are the days of a trip to the local zoo to see animals. With a field studies approach, students engage in targeted investigation, and any trip outside of class—to the zoo or elsewhere—is just one part of a larger learning experience.

Brad Olney's 4th grade class *does* go to the zoo—and often—as part of their field study of animal adaptation. "The zoo is part of my classroom," explained Mr. Olney, who purchases zoo passes for all of this students. "We read and write in the zoo, and we observe animal behaviors and come to understand adaptation. I could show videos of this, but my students would miss out on the social experience of interacting with other visitors. My students teach guests all about animal behavior and adaptation just as part of their own learning."

Ensuring authentic and applied learning experiences requires us to be mindful of the range of opportunities we provide that allow students to apply what they have learned in a broader way. For this reason, authentic and applied learning doesn't have to involve visits to community sites; it can take place inside the classroom just as well. For example, each year, the students in Marsha Van Landingham's statistics class investigate the propositions that are on the state ballot. Ms. Van Landingham has a series of questions about the propositions, and students have to use their knowledge of statistics, especially population statistics, to figure out the answers. In addition to the "ballot analysis" project, Ms. Van Landingham's students conduct original research. They develop a research question, identify a sample that they can use to collect data, and analyze their data statistically. The experiences the students have in Ms. Van Landingham's class allow them to apply their knowledge of statistics to issues that are occurring in the world around them.

We also believe that authentic learning requires that students understand their role as citizens in the learning community. There are many ways for teachers to provide students with opportunities to reflect on their citizenship. At Health Sciences High, students self-assess their actions each week using the rubric found in Figure 5.3. This rubric is available digitally, on the school's learning management system (LMS), and guides student reflection on their actions and whether or not these actions are consistent with who they want to be. The LMS captures students' reflections so that teachers can provide students with feedback. On a rotating basis, teachers talk with students about the actions that demonstrate various levels of learning in whole-group and individual conversations.

As we have noted, all students should have goals. They should know what they want to achieve and have plans for getting there. This requires that teachers spend time in their classrooms helping students clarify their goals and monitor progress toward those goals.

Every three weeks in Amanda Green's 6th grade classroom, students review their goals and write steps they've taken toward achieving them. The goals can relate to academic areas or not. For example, Sierra was focused on her reading fluency. As she said, "I read fast enough, but it doesn't really sound like talking. I want to be more fluent because that will help me in my acting." When students have goals, their teachers can make connections between those goals and class activities.

FIGURE 5.3
Citizenship Rubric

To receive a score, the student meets several, but not necessarily all, of the following criteria:

	Excellent	Good	Needs Improvement	Unacceptable
Welcome	• Responds positively to and takes action on feedback. • Demonstrates and models leadership qualities within the community (e.g., uses welcoming verbal and nonverbal communication; encourages others to be welcoming; mentors others to foster a welcoming environment). • Actively seeks out interaction with adults.	• Responds positively to feedback and frequently takes action on it. • Demonstrates a welcoming attitude toward others (e.g., verbal and nonverbal communication). • Interacts with adults regularly, and occasionally initiates contact.	• Inconsistently responds to and takes action on feedback. • Demonstrates welcoming attitude at times (e.g., verbal and nonverbal communication is at times less welcoming). • Interacts with adults positively when approached, but rarely initiates contact.	• Regularly struggles with feedback or fails to take action on the feedback given. • Makes others feel unwelcome. • Refuses to help others when requested; disrupts others and the learning environment. • Avoids contact with adults.
Do No Harm	• Demonstrates concern for others and the learning environment and models leadership qualities that improve circumstances. • Consistently and actively participates in and, at times, leads the restorative process. Contributions are insightful and advance the discussion. • Seeks adult assistance and intervention to prevent harm from occurring. • Consistently presents own work in class and encourages academic honesty in the learning community (e.g., does not allow others to copy his or her work, counsels others to make ethical academic decisions). • Consistently follows courtesy policy in regard to use of personal electronic devices, and anticipates when and how these devices are best used.	• Demonstrates concern for others and the learning environment and follows the lead of others to improve circumstances. • Consistently and willingly participates in and contributes meaningful ideas to the restorative process (circles, conferences, etc.). • Consistently presents own work in class and contributes to an ethical learning environment (e.g., does not allow others to copy his or her work). • Consistently follows teacher directions given regarding use of personal electronic devices.	• Often demonstrates concern for others and the learning environment. • Participates in the restorative process (circles, conferences, etc.). • Consistently presents own work in class and contributes to an ethical learning environment (e.g., does not allow others to copy his or her work). • Occasionally needs reminders or redirection regarding the use of personal electronic devices.	• Repeatedly does physical, verbal, or emotional harm to others or the learning environment. • Significantly disrupts the community (restoring harm to those hurt can result in change in citizenship). • Rarely or unwillingly participates in the restorative process (circles, conferences, etc.). • Submits plagiarized or copied work in class or allows others to copy his or her work. • Repeatedly uses personal learning devices despite teacher reminder and redirection.

FIGURE 5.3—(continued)
Citizenship Rubric

	Excellent	Good	Satisfactory	Unacceptable
Choice Words	• Consistently influences others by modeling positive and appropriate language. • Consistently communicates kindly with peers both in and out of the classroom. • Consistently uses academic language to express ideas in class discussions.	• Often models positive and appropriate language. • Often communicates kindly with peers both in and out of the classroom. • Strives to use academic language to express ideas in class discussions.	• Demonstrates understanding of appropriate and kind language, and strives to use it. • Occasionally uses language that degrades or belittles self or others, or is inappropriate for school, but understands its effects and consequences.	• Frequently uses language that degrades or belittles self or others. • Regularly uses inappropriate language (language that is not well-suited for school or academic settings). • Remains unaware of or resistant to the effects and consequences of harsh language despite adult guidance.
Never Too Late to Learn	• Attends 95% or more of the time. • Sets a scholarly example through careful preparation for learning (e.g., completing assignments, anticipating topics, bringing additional materials to contribute to class discussion). • Reliably present throughout class, and makes decisions to minimize effect of brief time out of class. • Constructive in groups as a member, regularly serving as a leader and promoting and supporting the leadership of others. • Can be relied upon to contribute to discussions to advance the learning of self and others by posing questions and making connections to other disciplines and subjects. • Reliably seeks resources or academic assistance in order to persevere (e.g., additional materials, academic recovery, tutoring, intervention, office hours, homework completion, etc.).	• Attends 95% or more of the time. • Comes to class on time and prepared intellectually and organizationally to learn (e.g., completed assignments, materials, completed out-of-class readings for discussion). • Frequently present throughout class, and often makes decisions to minimize effect of brief time out of class. • Constructive in groups, sometimes as a leader, and consistently as a member. • Frequently contributes to class discussions in ways that advance the learning of self and others, occasionally posing questions or making connections to other disciplines and subjects. • Frequently seeks resources or academic assistance with little or no prompting in order to persevere (e.g., additional materials, academic recovery, tutoring, intervention, office hours, homework completion, etc.).	• Attends 95% or more of the time. • Usually comes to class on time and prepared to learn (e.g., completed assignments, materials, completed out-of-class readings for discussion). • Usually present throughout class, although effect of time out of class is sometimes prolonged and requires teacher redirection. • Constructive in groups as a member. • Often contributes pertinent and on-topic information to class discussions. • Needs prompting and encouragement to seek resources or academic assistance in order to persevere (e.g., additional materials, academic recovery, tutoring, intervention, office hours, etc.).	• Attends < 95% of the time. • Often unprepared to learn, without assignments completed. • Often out of class for prolonged periods of time, negatively affecting his or her individual learning and that of the group. • Attitudes and/or contributions are counterproductive to the group and the learning environment. • Routinely inattentive to class discussions; rarely participates; often offers information that is off-topic. • Avoids accepting challenges. • Needs to be reminded to get help. Gives up easily. Does not take advantage of help offered. • Needs continuous redirection and/or attention. Routinely needs to be reminded to put non-classroom materials away and return to a learning state.

Source: Health Sciences High & Middle College. Used with permission.

First Steps: It Starts with You

Beyond what you learned during first-week-of-school activities designed to get to know one another, do you have any idea what your students aspire to? (We don't mean just the handful of them who talk with you all the time; we mean all of your students.) If you don't, start there. Find out what each student aspires to in terms of occupation and education. Then meet with them individually and have a short conference about their goals. Make a point of checking in with them, perhaps each quarter, to discuss their progress. Use this information in parent-teacher conferences, and when you're representing a student in a school meeting. How can we be dream managers for them if we don't know the dreams of each one of them?

Conclusion

Ian's earliest recollection of his father's law office was a framed black and white cartoon of a man relaxing behind a desk—leaning back with his feet up and hands behind his head. The caption underneath read, "We pay on results, not effort." In this chapter, we proposed the notion that our work to create more effective and equitable schools must be judged by the results of our actions. *Ultimately, equity must be measured in the learning, not the teaching.* We aspire to equity at the finish line, not just the starting line. Our school equity work is designed to produce engaged and inspired learners. We know we can achieve that for a few. But can we do it for all? To repeat the criteria shared at the beginning of this chapter, can we ensure an entire student body

- Who are capable and accomplished learners?
- Who are continuously building and reinforcing their identity and agency?
- Who have been empowered to use and direct their education toward exploring and pursuing their interests, skills, and aspirations?
- Whose dreams are complemented with viable action plans and opportunities?

The move to this highest level in the equity taxonomy is predicated on previously discussed conditions:

- The physical integration of students in quality schools.
- The welcoming climate that supports students' agency and identity through the way we talk to them.
- The structural access to curriculum that ensures challenging courses for all.
- The grading systems that focus on mastery, not just performance.
- Instructional excellence that is structured so that students learn, not just absorb, content.

The physical, social, psychological, and academic milieu communicates volumes to our students each day. A growth mindset is enhanced or diminished based on these effects. And while individual talented teachers open up possibilities to children, it is systems that magnify their effect.

CHAPTER 6

From Acquisition to Action
The Review, the Audit, and Beyond

We have presented a lot of information in the previous five chapters. And you may be saying to yourself, "Where do I start?" For many, the task of improving equity is daunting, even paralyzing. We recommend you start with the Building Equity Review, focusing on the 25 statements we've explored in this book. Identify strengths that you can build on and areas for growth. There are any number of ways, and places, to start. But nothing will be gained by waiting another day to take the next step in the equity journey.

We'll highlight the plan, and the journey, at our school, emphasizing that it is but one example of the process you could use.

The equity plan we created at our school was grounded in Instructional Excellence, which is Level 4 of the Building Equity Taxonomy. We made the decision to start there for several reasons. First of all, instructional excellence has long been a foundational focus of our school. We have common language and expectations for instruction that were created around staff development and guided by the Framework for Intentional and Targeted Teaching (Fisher, Frey, & Hite, 2016). We wanted our equity plan to evolve from our focus on instruction rather than compete with it. In other words, because we already shared an approach to instructional improvement, we believed many of the needs that were identified and the actions that were proposed through our equity audit could be addressed via our plans for excellent curriculum and instruction. Of course, other schools might start in other places.

The second reason we embedded our equity plan within instructional excellence is because we have spent several years coming to agreements about school culture and academic intent. Notably, we understand as a staff that while agreements about high-quality instruction are necessary, they are also insufficient for actually building a culture of achievement or ensuring equity for all students. To complement high-quality instruction, we have engaged in considerable social-emotional learning, including a focus on establishing and maintaining healthy, growth-producing relationships between staff and students. As a result, we have structured our professional learning to link our social-emotional learning efforts with instructional excellence. We believed that our equity plan could be embedded nicely into that existing structure.

Finally, engaging in the full Building Equity Audit allowed us to identify our areas of greatest need and propose activities in two different levels of the Building Equity Taxonomy. Interestingly, neither of the two targeted levels were instructional excellence.

Now you must be confused! Let us explain. When we analyzed our survey evidence, we saw that most of our equity issues were at Level 3: Opportunities to Learn, and at Level 5: Engaged and Inspired Learners. This suggested that there was a group of students who were still lacking the supports they needed to more fully engage as active school citizens and learners. It also suggested that there was a second group of students who were engaged but whom we needed to advance as empowered learners. We felt that by reexamining our instructional practices, we could incorporate additional actions to more effectively meet both the social-emotional needs of students and advance student voice, aspirations, and empowerment.

We share our experience here to emphasize that the best way to introduce new schoolwide initiatives is to build them upon the strengths and structures that are already present. It is important to look at the foundations you have—what agreements, norms, and structures are currently in place to manage schoolwide initiatives. If those are effective, use them to conduct your Building Equity Review and to construct and execute your equity plan. If your school site is lacking an effective school improvement infrastructure, then the review may help you simultaneously build your equity plan and your school improvement infrastructure. Of course, you can also use the full Building Equity Audit, especially if you have already begun the focus on equity within your classroom, school, or district.

One aspect of our equity plan was to create a "dream team" of teacher leaders. Every member of the team was a National Board–certified teacher. They were charged with identifying ways to build and infuse student voice, student agency, and student aspiration throughout our integrated college- and career-prep curriculum. One of the structural features they proposed was an eight-month rotation through specific discussion prompts. They recommended that the prompts be used schoolwide, the same way we use our essential questions. Specifically, grade levels would make decisions about creating lessons and activities that would feature reading and writing, and present prompt-specific reflections. Staff would then highlight and feature prompt-related products through our social media, in our morning circles, on our walls, and in our classrooms. The prompts included the following:

September: *I am...*
October: *I aspire to be...*
November: *My well-being, physical, emotional...*
December/January: *I contributed... I am challenged by...*
February: *My heart beats for... I wake up in the morning for... I am motivated by...*
March: *I want to explore...*
April: *I will know I am successful when...*
May: *I have grown—I have accomplished...*

Our mathematics department leader, Joseph Assof, challenged his Math 3 class to use the September *I am...* prompt to describe themselves through a mathematical function. Figure 6.1 shows three of the many wonderful products the students completed.

FIGURE 6.1
Mathematical Responses to "I Am..."

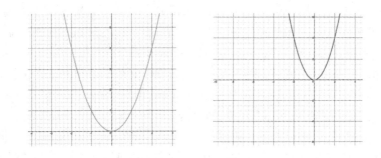

Alyza Crucena

I am a quadratic function. The left-end behavior reflects the right-end behavior, similar to how my decisions affect my future. When I'm negative, my attitude is upside down, just like the parabola $y = -x^2$. When I'm positive, my attitude makes me smile in the shape of the parabola $y = x^2$. I always try to do my best to be happy, even when I hit rock bottom of (0,0). The negative people in my life try to drag me down to feel as little as negative infinity. So I surround myself with only positive, boosting me to infinity. No one can restrict me from what I want to be. All real numbers? More like all real dreams. I am Alyza Crucena.

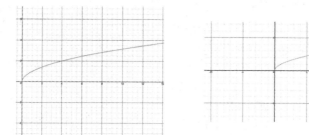

Isela Gutierrez

I am a square root function. Like the square root, I too have another half. I am like its increases: as the roots grow, so does my knowledge. Like its origin, I too started at zero on September 4, 1999. I am like its range because I have infinite potential. Like the square root, you should not plug in anything negative because I blow up. I only surround myself with positivity. As I get further in life, I feel like I work more for less success. I may never reach the end, but I stay positive with each step closer. I am Isela Gutierrez.

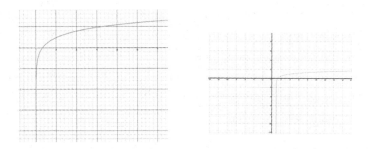

Andrea Marquez

I am a logarithmic function. Feeling down and knowing it would never come to an end. Slowly changing my mind and coming up. I finally crossed the line, and knew I wanted to go up. Nothing will bring me down again after I cross the line. I keep moving forward, but I stay consistent in the same direction. Just like my right-end behavior, I'm always approaching infinite positivity. I am Andrea Marquez.

Using This Book

The Building Equity Taxonomy and Building Equity Review presented in this book are intended to provoke schoolwide conversations and, we hope, lead to further inquiry via the Building Equity Audit and to schoolwide agreements, commitments, and actions. Ultimately, we would like to see these agreements, commitments, and actions become part of every school's goals and vision to become a more effective and equitable school. Here's what we have done to facilitate this process.

1. We introduced the Building Equity Taxonomy as a means of categorizing and organizing various types of equity needs and initiatives.
2. We aligned the chapters of this book to the levels of the BET and presented 25 foundational statements to call attention to first steps of equity inquiry. The inputs and practices discussed in each chapter are intended to spark ideas responsive to the needs identified by your review.
3. We created two versions (teacher and student) of the full Building Equity Audit, which are available for download online (see Appendixes

A and B). The audit involves using surveys to collect evidence of a school's equity accomplishments and shortcomings. We constructed the audit surveys in alignment with the levels of the taxonomy so that the taxonomy is a means of organizing the data in order to generate a functional audit and to focus resulting schoolwide agreements, commitments, and actions.

As previously mentioned, most schools already have established structures for how schoolwide initiatives like this are organized and implemented. Our own school typically relies on a professional learning community (PLC) process to bring together a diverse group to study, discuss, and develop understanding and expertise. For example, we formed several collaborative planning teams to read drafts of this book, and during the resulting discussions, members became resolute in recommending to the school leadership that we engage in an audit of our own. They proposed a professional learning session to highlight the content and recommended a process for completing the two versions of the Building Equity Audit. When the data were in, we facilitated a second whole-staff session to provide data disaggregated by each level of the taxonomy. Collaborative planning teams then worked to identify evidence that provoked concern and demanded attention. They summarized the results of those discussions and identified areas of common concerns. They then prepared a set of recommendations for a series of follow-up activities and equity-based practices to respond to these common concerns. The proposed plan was shared with staff in order to confirm our agreements, commitments, and planned actions.

Conducting the Building Equity Audit

Of course, we would love to see a universal set of equity audit procedures develop so that student, educator, and parent data could be collected and compared across schools on a large scale. This will probably happen one day, but it is secondary to encouraging each school to use the Building Equity Review and Building Equity Audit to collect and organize data in a way that is most useful to them. For example, some schools will want to code and disaggregate data by grade level or by credentialed and certified staff, whereas other schools will see value in aggregated schoolwide data. We are aware of an elementary school that chose to cut, edit, and rewrite the items on the student version of the Building Equity Audit. This meant teachers could choose a selected statement for class discussion in order to reach agreement on the statement's meaning before distributing the entire survey.

Finally, we believe schools will find the results of both the teacher and student versions informative, but in our experience, some of the most interesting conversations surface when examining responses across the versions. For example, what does it mean if 80 percent of teachers affirm that they believe students know they care about them, but results of the student version show that only 38 percent of the students believe their teachers care about them? That discrepancy might provide insights about what is working and what isn't and suggest alternative courses of action.

In our school, conducting the audit was pretty straightforward, because our model for continuous program improvement is established and transparent. Our technology team put the student and teacher versions online, and we made a decision to have them completed in each social studies class. We then set aside time and put structures in place to analyze the data, and we set up task teams to implement and manage our agreed-upon actions.

Conclusion

The 25 statements of the Building Equity Review highlight foundational equity-focused policies and practices. They are essential considerations for all school staff who are committed to ensuring every student receives an education that is worthy of his or her boundless possibilities. It makes sense, then, that these 25 statements also appear in the staff version of the full Building Equity Audit. They help generate part of the picture, but not the whole.

Because the vision of our equity work is to foster a more empowered, engaged, and inspired student body, it seems appropriate to now consider items from the student version of the survey related to assessing student empowerment. Review the list below and ask yourself what percentage of your student body could affirm a majority of these statements:

1. I am proud of myself.
2. I like who I am.
3. I know where I am going.
4. I don't feel lost.
5. I am very positive about my future.
6. School is a place that is helping me dream about my future.
7. School is a place that is helping me plan my future.
8. School is giving me positive power.
9. I like what I am learning.
10. I've got a plan for myself.
11. I am prepared to work hard to reach my dreams.
12. I feel I have lots of chances to ask and answer questions about myself.
13. School is helping me discover what life is all about.
14. School is helping me discover what I am all about.
15. I am a leader.
16. I feel empowered as a student.
17. I am a powerful person.
18. I feel prepared to face the challenges in my life.
19. I can look in the mirror and smile at who I see.
20. I have wonderful dreams about my future.
21. Some of the things I learn in school help me dream bigger.
22. I learn more about myself every year.
23. I don't feel held back.
24. Nothing is going to keep me from reaching my goals.
25. I have aspirations.

Hold in your mind the percentage of your school's students that you believe would respond affirmatively to these statements. Now, here's a set of questions for you to answer:

- Is your guess/estimate comforting or concerning to you?
- Are you interested in finding out what the percentage really is?
- Do you see a more engaged and inspired student body as a reasonable outcome of finding out?
- Are your students' responses to these items important to you?
- Are your goals and vision of your individual and collective work focused on making your school more effective and equitable?
- Would your colleagues answer these questions differently from you?
- What would it take to create a schoolwide conversation about the interest and importance of creating a more engaged and inspired student body?

And so, we ask you: *What are your next steps?* There is no bad place to start. But we do hope that you will take the first step and strive for improved opportunities for all students. Each of them deserves a fair shot, and this requires an education that is both equal and equitable.

Appendix A: The Building Equity Audit—Staff Version

A copy of this survey is available for download at **www.ascd.org/ASCD/ pdf/books/smith2017BEAstaff.pdf**. Use the password **"Equity117031"** to unlock the PDF.

PHYSICAL INTEGRATION

1. Our student body is diverse.
2. Students are being prepared to function as members of a diverse society.
3. Our school publicly seeks and values a diverse student body.
4. We reach out to families from different backgrounds to ensure they feel welcomed and valued.
5. Efforts are made to promote students' respecting, and interacting with, students from different backgrounds.
6. There are tensions in the school between students with different backgrounds and identities.
7. Our school facilities and resources are at least equal to those of other district schools.
8. We are proud of our school facilities and resources.
9. Classroom placement and student schedules ensure that diversity exists in all learning environments.
10. There are self-contained or special day classes on our campus.

SOCIAL-EMOTIONAL ENGAGEMENT

11. The social and emotional needs of students—from prosocial skills to responsiveness to trauma—are adequately supported in our school.
12. Students feel safe at school.
13. Teachers know what to do if a student's mental health and well-being are in question.
14. Students who need counseling and social services receive them.
15. Bullying is not a problem at our school.
16. There are students who are afraid to come to school.
17. Teachers and staff show they care about students.
18. We care for, support, and mentor some students beyond their classroom performance.
19. Students have at least one adult in school who cares about, supports, and mentors them.
20. We promote positive race and human relations to better understand and interact with students from different backgrounds.
21. We are a culturally competent staff.
22. Our school has programs and policies that are designed to improve attendance.
23. We need to spend more time trying to improve attendance.
24. Our school's discipline plans are restorative rather than punitive.
25. Staff receive professional development to help us understand and implement our schoolwide discipline plan.
26. We understand and support our schoolwide approach to discipline.
27. Students value their relationships with teachers.
28. Students are treated equitably when they misbehave, and consequences are based on an ethic of care rather than demographic characteristics.
29. Students from specific subgroups are treated differently than others when they misbehave.
30. Students from specific subgroups are more likely to be sent out of class, suspended, or expelled.

OPPORTUNITY TO LEARN

31. We do not use tracking to group or schedule students.
32. There is a noticeable relationship between student demographics and challenging assignments and classes.
33. We have remedial classes.
34. We have two sets of core classes: high level and basic.
35. Students have equitable access to class placement and course offerings.
36. Students are encouraged to take on challenging classes, projects, and activities.
37. All students have access to challenging curriculum.
38. We pay attention to differentiation and are well prepared to differentiate our instruction.
39. I am able to meet the needs of a diverse group of students.
40. We have interventions in place to help our students succeed in our core classes.
41. Teachers have high expectations for all students.
42. Students know we believe in them and that they are capable of challenging work.
43. We need remedial classes.
44. There are active working relationships between home and school to increase opportunities to learn.
45. Parents know we believe their children are capable of great things.
46. We communicate positively, regularly, and promptly with families.
47. We invite families to get involved in school events and decision making.
48. Parents know how their child's schedule meets standards and is preparing their child for the next school level.
49. Soft skills are developed and valued in our school.

INSTRUCTIONAL EXCELLENCE

50. Students are demonstrating commitment, perseverance, and flexibility, especially in challenging situations.
51. Students are learning to manage their time and complete tasks.

52. We build creativity and problem-solving skills.

53. Our students learn how to communicate, collaborate, and work in small groups.

54. All students experience quality core instruction.

55. Students in every classroom experience focused instruction, guided instruction, collaborative learning, and independent learning every day.

56. Teachers actively convey the learning purposes in every lesson.

57. Students understand criteria for success in every classroom.

58. There are transparent and transportable instructional routines in place schoolwide.

59. Grading and progress reports are focused on subject matter mastery and competence.

60. Teachers notice students' individual instructional needs and have systems to differentiate as needed.

61. I am aware of and support our school's response to intervention program.

62. Flexible heterogeneous and homogenous small groups meet daily in classrooms.

63. We have access to professional learning that builds our technical and intellectual skills.

64. Our professional learning highlights teaching and learning and is aligned to our school's academic goals.

65. Instructional coaching is available to every teacher.

ENGAGED AND INSPIRED LEARNERS

66. Students are engaged in a wide range of leadership activities within our school.

67. Student aspirations are fostered.

68. Students select learning opportunities related to their interests.

69. Students are provided authentic and applied learning experiences that link with their goals and aspirations.

70. Students are inspired by their teachers to achieve greatness.

Most of our students will agree with the following statements:

71. I am proud of myself.
72. I like who I am.
73. I know where I am going.
74. I don't feel lost.
75. I am positive about my future.
76. School is a place that is helping me dream about my future.
77. School is a place that is helping me plan my future.
78. School is giving me positive power.
79. I like what I am learning.
80. I've got a plan for myself.
81. I am prepared to work hard to reach my dreams.
82. I feel I have lots of chances to ask and answer questions about myself.
83. School is helping me discover what life is all about.
84. School is helping me discover what I am all about.
85. I am a leader.
86. I feel empowered as a student.
87. I am a powerful person.
88. I feel prepared to face the challenges in my life.
89. I can look in the mirror and smile at who I see.
90. I have wonderful dreams about my future.
91. Some of the things I learn in school help me dream bigger.
92. I learn more about myself every year.
93. I don't feel held back.
94. Nothing is going to keep me from reaching my goals.
95. I have aspirations.

Appendix B: The Building Equity Audit—Student Version

A copy of this survey is available for download at **www.ascd.org/ASCD/pdf/books/smith2017BEAstudent.pdf**. Use the password **"Equity117031"** to unlock the PDF.

PHYSICAL INTEGRATION

1. Our student body is diverse.
2. I am being prepared to function as a member of a diverse society.
3. School staff reach out to my family to ensure they feel welcomed and valued.
4. Students respect, and interact with, students from different backgrounds.
5. There are tensions in the school between students with different backgrounds and identities.
6. Staff understand my culture and background.
7. I am proud of my school and our school facilities and resources.
8. Students who need extra supports get them in our classrooms instead of in special classes.

SOCIAL-EMOTIONAL ENGAGEMENT

9. I feel safe at school.
10. My mental health needs are being met at school.
11. Bullying is not a problem at our school.
12. I know students who are afraid to come to school.

13. I believe staff care about me.
14. Staff care for, support, and mentor students beyond their classroom performance.
15. I know at least one adult in school who cares about, supports, and mentors me.
16. Staff care whether I am at school or not.
17. Our teachers and administrators want students to learn from the good and bad choices we make.
18. I understand and support our schoolwide approach to discipline.
19. I value my relationships with teachers.
20. Students from specific subgroups are treated differently than others when they misbehave.

OPPORTUNITY TO LEARN

21. It seems like students are placed in classes and groups based on race, culture, ability, or identity.
22. Students are encouraged to take on challenging classes, projects, and activities.
23. I am challenged in my classes.
24. Teachers seem to be able to meet the needs of all their students, including me.
25. Teachers have high expectations for me. They believe in me and my abilities.
26. I feel my family and school are working together to help me succeed.
27. School staff share my accomplishments with my family.
28. My parents are aware that I am being prepared for the future.

INSTRUCTIONAL EXCELLENCE

29. I am encouraged to demonstrate commitment, perseverance, and flexibility, especially in challenging situations.
30. I am learning to manage my time and to complete tasks.
31. I am learning to be more creative and to solve problems.
32. I am learning how to communicate, collaborate, and work in groups.
33. I believe I am receiving excellent instruction in my classes.

34. Teachers make me aware of the learning purpose in every lesson.
35. I understand what is required to be successful in each of my classes.
36. Teachers notice and meet students' individual instructional needs.
37. I am able to work with lots of different students in small groups.

ENGAGED AND INSPIRED LEARNERS

38. There are lots of leadership opportunities for students at my school.
39. Staff provide me opportunities based on knowing my interests.
40. I think our school connects me to real-world issues and experiences.
41. I am proud of myself.
42. I like who I am.
43. I know where I am going.
44. I don't feel lost.
45. I am positive about my future.
46. School is a place that is helping me dream about my future.
47. School is a place that is helping me plan my future.
48. School is giving me positive power.
49. I like what I am learning.
50. I've got a plan for myself.
51. I am prepared to work hard to reach my dreams.
52. I feel I have lots of chances to ask and answer questions about myself.
53. School is helping me discover what life is all about.
54. School is helping me discover what I am all about.
55. I am a leader.
56. I feel empowered as a student.
57. I am a powerful person.
58. I feel prepared to face the challenges in my life.
59. I can look in the mirror and smile at who I see.
60. I have wonderful dreams about my future.
61. Some of the things I learn in school help me dream bigger.
62. I learn more about myself every year.
63. I don't feel held back.
64. Nothing is going to keep me from reaching my goals.
65. I have aspirations.

References

Alexander, K. (2014). *The crossover.* New York: Houghton Mifflin Harcourt.

Allen, J., Gregory, A., Mikami, A., Lun, J., Hamre, B., & Pianta, R. (2013). Observations of effective teacher-student interactions in secondary classrooms: Predicting student achievement with the Classroom Assessment Scoring System—Secondary. *School Psychology Review, 42*(1), 76–98.

Allensworth, E. M., & Easton, J. Q. (2007). *What matters for staying on-track and graduating in Chicago public high schools: A close look at course grades, failures, and attendance in the freshman year.* Chicago: University of Chicago, Consortium on Chicago School Research.

American School Counselor Association. (2017). *The ASCA national model: A framework for school counseling programs* (3rd ed.). Alexandria, VA: ASCA.

Andrews, A. (2014). *Some assembly required: The not-so-secret life of a transgender teen.* New York: Simon & Schuster Books for Young Readers.

Balfanz, R., & Byrnes, V. (2012). *The importance of being in school: A report on absenteeism in the nation's public schools.* Baltimore: Johns Hopkins University Center for Social Organization of Schools.

Balfanz, R., Byrnes, V., & Fox, J. (2013, April 6). *Sent home and put off track: The antecedents, disproportionalities, and consequences of being suspended in the ninth grade.* Paper presented at the Closing the School Discipline Gap: Research to Practice Conference, Washington, DC.

Barrett, S., Eber, L., & Weist, M. (Eds.). (2009). *Advancing education effectiveness: Interconnecting school mental health and school-wide positive behavior support.* Washington, DC: U.S. Department of Education Office of Special Education Programs.

Beam, C. (2012). *I am J.* New York: Little, Brown Books for Young Readers.

Becker, B. E., & Luthar, S. S. (2002). Social-emotional factors affecting achievement outcomes among disadvantaged students: Closing the achievement gap. *Educational Psychologist, 37*(4), 197–214.

Block, P. (2008). *Community: The structure of belonging.* Oakland, CA: Berrett-Koehler Publishers .

Byrnes, D., & Yamamoto, K. (1985). Academic retention: An inside look. *Education, 106,* 208–214.

California Department of Education. (2016, September 29). *Fingertip facts on education in California–CalEdFacts.* Retrieved from http://www.cde.ca.gov/ds/sd/cb/ceffingertipfacts.asp

Carroll, J. B. (1963). A model of school learning. *Teachers College Record, 64,* 723–733.

Clinedinst, M. (2015). *State of college admission.* Arlington, VA: National Association for College Admission Counseling. Retrieved from http://www.nxtbook.com/ygsreprints/NACAC/2014SoCA_nxtbk/#/0

Coleman, A. L., Negrón, F. M. Jr., & Lipper, K. E. (2014). *Achieving educational excellence for all: A guide to diversity-related policy strategies for school districts.* Alexandria, VA: National School Boards Association.

Collaborative for Academic, Social, and Emotional Learning. (2015). *2015 CASEL guide: Effective social and emotional learning programs—Middle and high school edition.* Retrieved from http://www.casel.org/middle-and-high-school-edition-casel-guide/

Costello, B., Wachtel, J., & Wachtel, T. (2009). *The restorative practices handbook for teachers, disciplinarians, and administrators.* Bethlehem, PA: International Institute for Restorative Practices.

Crenshaw, K. (1989). Demarginalizing the intersection of race and sex: A black feminist critique of antidiscrimination doctrine, feminist theory, and antiracist politics. *The University of Chicago Legal Forum, 1989*(1), 139–167.

Derrington, M. L., & Angelle, P. S. (2013). Teacher leadership and collective efficacy: Connections and links. *International Journal of Teacher Leadership, 4*(1), 1–13.

Donovan, M. S., & Bransford, J. D. (Eds.). (2005). *How students learn: History, mathematics, and science in the classroom.* Committee on How People Learn: A Targeted Report for Teachers. Division on Behavioral and Social Sciences and Education. Washington, DC: National Academies.

DuFour, R., DuFour, R., Eaker, R., & Many, T. (2010). *Learning by doing: A handbook for professional communities at work—A practical guide for PLC teams and leadership.* Bloomington, IN: Solution Tree.

Dweck, C. S. (2007). *Mindset: The new psychology of success.* New York: Ballantine.

Dweck, C. S. (2015, September 23). Growth mindset, revisited. *Education Week, 35*(5), 20, 24.

Eccles, J. (2009). Who am I and what am I going to do with my life? Personal and collective identities as motivators of action. *Educational Psychologist, 44*(2), 78–89.

Epstein, J. L., Sanders, M. G., Simon, B. S., Salinas, K. C., Jansorn, N. R., & Van Voorhis, F. L. (2002). *School, family, and community partnerships: Your handbook for action* (2nd ed.). Thousand Oaks, CA: Corwin.

Fazel, M., Hoagwood, K., Stephan, S., & Ford, T. (2014). Mental health interventions in schools 1: Mental health interventions in high-income countries. *Lancet Psychiatry, 1*(5), 377–387.

Fisher, D., & Frey, N. (2003). *Inclusive urban schools.* Baltimore: Paul H. Brookes.

Fisher, D., & Frey, N. (2010). *Guided instruction: How to develop confident and successful learners.* Alexandria, VA: ASCD.

Fisher, D., & Frey, N. (2011). *The purposeful classroom: How to structure lessons with learning goals in mind.* Alexandria, VA: ASCD.

Fisher, D., & Frey, N. (2014). *Better learning through structured teaching: A framework for the gradual release of responsibility* (2nd ed.). Alexandria, VA: ASCD.

Fisher, D., Frey, N., & Hattie, J. (2016). *Visible learning for literacy, grades K–12: Implementing the practices that work best to accelerate student learning.* Thousand Oaks, CA: Corwin.

Fisher, D., Frey, N., & Hite, S. A. (2016). *Intentional and targeted teaching: A framework for teacher growth and leadership.* Alexandria, VA: ASCD.

Fisher, D., Frey, N., & Lapp, D. (2009). Meeting AYP in a high-need school: A formative experiment. *Journal of Adolescent and Adult Literacy, 52,* 386–396.

Fisher, D., Frey, N., & Pumpian, I. (2011, November). No penalties for practice. *Educational Leadership, 69*(3), 46–51.

Fisher, D., Frey, N., &, Pumpian, I. (2012). *How to create a culture of achievement in your school and classroom.* Alexandria, VA: ASCD.

Fisher, D., Frey, N., & Williams, D. (2002, November). Seven literacy strategies that work. *Educational Leadership, 60*(3), 70–73.

Garmezy, N., Masten, A. S. & Tellegen, A. (1984). The study of stress and competence in children: A building block for developmental psychopathology. *Child Development, 55,* 97–111.

Garrett, R., & Hong, G. (2016). Impacts of grouping and time on the math learning of language minority kindergartners. *Educational Evaluation and Policy Analysis, 38*(2), 222–244.

Goddard, R. D., Hoy, W. K., & Woolfolk Hoy, A. (2000). Collective efficacy: Its meaning, measure, and impact on student achievement. *American Educational Research Journal, 37,* 479–507.

Goddard, Y. L., Goddard, R. D., & Tschannen-Moran, M. (2007). A theoretical and empirical investigation of teacher collaboration for school improvement and student achievement in public elementary schools. *Teachers College Record, 109*(4), 877–896.

Gulamhussein, A. (2013). *Teaching the teachers: Effective professional development in an era of high stakes accountability.* Center for Public Education and the National School Boards Association. Retrieved from http://www.centerforpubliceducation.org/Main-Menu/Staffingstudents/Teaching-the-Teachers-Effective-Professional-Development-in-an-Era-of-High-Stakes-Accountability/Teaching-the-Teachers-Full-Report.pdf

Guskey, T. (2014). *On your mark: Challenging the conventions of grading and reporting.* Bloomington, IN: Solution Tree.

Hattie, J. (2009). *Visible learning: A synthesis of over 800 meta-analyses relating to achievement.* New York: Routledge.

Hattie, J. (2012). *Visible learning for teachers: Maximizing impact on learning.* New York: Routledge.

Hattie, J. (2015). The applicability of visible learning to higher education. *Scholarship of Teaching and Learning in Psychology, 1*(1), 79–91.

Hattie, J. A., & Timperley, H. (2007). The power of feedback. *Review of Educational Research, 77,* 81–112.

Heitink, M. C., Van der Kleij, F. M., Veldkamp, B. P., Schildkamp, K., & Kippers, W. B. (2016, February). A systematic review of prerequisites for implementing assessment for learning in classroom practice. *Education Research Review, 17,* 50–62.

Henderson, N. (2013, September). Havens of resilience. *Educational Leadership, 71*(1), 22–27.

Henson, J., & Gilles, C. (2003). Al's story: Overcoming beliefs that inhibit learning. *Language Arts, 80*(4), 259–267.

Horrigan, J. B., & Duggan, M. (2015). *Home broadband 2015: The share of Americans with broadband at home has plateaued, and more rely only on their smartphones for access.* Washington, DC: Pew Research Center. Retrieved from http://www.pewinternet.org/files/2015/12/Broadband-adoption-full.pdf

Huang, R., & Li, Y. (2012). What matters most: A comparison of expert and novice teachers' noticing of mathematics classroom events. *School Science and Mathematics, 112*(7), 420–432.

Ingraham, C. L., Hokoda, A., Moehlenbruck, D., Karafin, M., Manzo, C., & Ramirez, D. (2016). Consultation and collaboration to develop and implement restorative practices in a culturally and linguistically diverse elementary school. *Journal of Educational and Psychological Consultation, 26*(4), 354–384.

Jefferson, T. (1787). From Thomas Jefferson to James Madison, 20 December 1787. Washington, DC: Founders Online, National Archives. Retrieved from http://founders.archives.gov/documents/Jefferson/01-12-02-0454. In J. P. Boyd (Ed.), *The papers of Thomas Jefferson,* 1955, vol. 12 (pp. 438–443). Princeton, NJ: Princeton University Press.

Jimerson, S. R., Anderson, G. E., & Whipple, A. D. (2002). Winning the battle and losing the war: Examining the relation between grade retention and dropping out of high school. *Psychology in the Schools, 39*(4), 441–457.

Johnston, P. (2004). *Choice words: How our language affects children's learning.* York, ME: Stenhouse.

Jones, S. R., & McEwen, M. K. (2000). A conceptual model of multiple dimensions of identity. *Journal of College Student Development, 41*(4), 405–414.

Kelly, M. (2007). *The dream manager.* New York: Hyperion.

Kennedy-Lewis, B. L., & Murphy, A. S. (2016). Listening to "frequent flyers": What persistently disciplined students have to say about being labeled as "bad." *Teachers College Record, 118*(1), 1–40.

Kirsch, I. S., Braun, H. I., Lennon, M. L., & Sands, A. M. (2016). *Choosing our future: A story of opportunity in America..* Princeton, NJ: ETS Center for Research on Human Capital and Education.

Kohli, S. (2014, November 18). Modern-day segregation in public schools. *The Atlantic.* Retrieved from https://www.theatlantic.com/education/archive/2014/11/modern-day-segregation-in-public-schools/382846/

Kohn, A. (1999). *Punished by rewards: The trouble with gold stars, incentive plans, A's, praise, and other bribes.* Boston: Houghton Mifflin.

Krathwohl, D. R. (2002). A revision of Bloom's taxonomy: An overview. *Theory into Practice, 41*(4), 212–218.

Ladson-Billings, G. (1995). Toward a theory of culturally relevant pedagogy. *American Educational Research Journal, 32*(3), 465–491.

Lafontaine, D., Baye, A., Vieluf, S., & Monseur, C. (2015). Equity in opportunity-to-learn and achievement in reading: A secondary analysis of PISA 2009 data. *Studies in Educational Evaluation, 47,* 1–11.

Latimer, J., Dowden, C., & Muise, D. (2005). The effectiveness of restorative justice practices: A meta-analysis. *Prison Journal, 85*(2), 127–144.

Lindsey, D. B., Kearney, K. M., Estrada, D., Terrell, R. D., & Lindsey, R. B. (2015). *A culturally proficient response to the Common Core: Ensuring equity through professional learning.* Thousand Oaks, CA: Corwin.

Lindsey, R. B., Robins, K. N., & Terrell, R. D. (2009). *Cultural proficiency: A manual for school leaders* (3rd ed.). Thousand Oaks, CA: Corwin.

Maslow, A. H. (1954). *Motivation and personality.* New York: Harper.

McTighe, J., & Wiggins, G. (2013). *Essential questions: Opening doors to student understanding.* Alexandria, VA: ASCD.

MetLife. (2007). *The MetLife survey of the American teacher: The homework experience.* Retrieved from https://www.metlife.com/assets/cao/contributions/foundation/american-teacher/metlife-survey-american-teacher-2007-homework-experience.pdf

Mobin-Uddin, A. (2005). *My name is Bilal.* Honesdale, PA: Boyds Mill Press.

Morisano, D., & Locke, E. A. (2013). Goal setting and academic achievement. In J. Hattie and E. M. Anderman (Eds.), *International handbook of student achievement* (pp. 45–48). New York: Routledge.

Nathan, M. J., & Petrosino, A. (2003). Expert blind spot among preservice teachers. *American Educational Research Journal, 40*(4), 905–928.

National Equity Project. (n.d.). Home page. Retrieved from http://nationalequityproject.org

National Institutes of Health. (2016). *Any disorder among children.* Retrieved from https://www.nimh.nih.gov/health/statistics/prevalence/any-disorder-among-children.shtml

National School Climate Center. (n.d.). *School climate.* Retrieved from http://www.schoolclimate.org/climate/

Oakes, J. (1985). *Keeping track: How schools structure inequality.* New Haven, CT: Yale University Press.

Organisation for Economic Co-operation and Development. (2010). *PISA 2009 results: Executive summary.* Retrieved from https://www.oecd.org/pisa/pisaproducts/46619703.pdf

P21 Partnership for 21st Century Learning. (2015). *The 4Cs research series.* Retrieved from http://www.p21.org/our-work/4cs-research-series

Payne, A. A., & Welch, K. (2015). Restorative justice in schools: The influence of race on restorative discipline. *Youth & Society, 47*(4), 539–564.

Pearson, P. D., & Gallagher, M. C. (1983). The instruction of reading comprehension. *Contemporary Educational Psychology, 8,* 317–344.

Peters, J. A. (2004). *Luna.* New York: Little, Brown Books for Young Readers.

Popham, W. J. (2011). *Classroom assessment: What teachers need to know* (6th ed.). Boston: Pearson.

Purkey, W. W., & Stanley, P. H. (1991). *Invitational teaching, learning, and living.* Washington, DC: National Education Association Library.

Rathmann, P. (1995). *Officer Buckle and Gloria.* New York: Putnam.

Redfield, S. E., & Kraft, T. (2012). What color is special education? *Journal of Law & Education, 41*(1), 129–200.

Reeves, D. B. (2008, November). The learning leader: Leadership for student empowerment. *Educational Leadership, 66*(3), 84–85.

Regents of the University of California. (2015). *A–g subject requirements.* Retrieved from http://www.ucop.edu/agguide/a-g-requirements/index.html

Riddle, P. A. (2013). *Contexts matter: The relationship between schoolwide student demographics and graduation rates.* (Doctoral dissertation). Retrieved from ProQuest Dissertations and Theses database. (UMI No. 3561392).

Rosenthal, R., & Jacobson, L. (1968). Pygmalion in the classroom. *The Urban Review, 3,* 16–20.

Ross, R. (2013). School climate and equity. In T. Dary and T. Pickeral (Eds.), *School climate practices for implementation and sustainability: A school climate practice brief, number 1* (pp. 39–42). New York: National School Climate Center.

Shifrer, D., Callahan, R. M., & Muller, C. (2013). Equity or marginalization? The high school course-taking of students labeled with a learning disability. *American Educational Research Journal, 50*(4), 656–682.

Silberglitt, B., Appleton, J. J., Burns, M. K., & Jimerson, S. R. (2006). Examining the effects of grade retention on student reading performance: A longitudinal study. *Journal of School Psychology, 44*(4), 255–270.

Simmons, J. (2003, May). Responders are taught, not born. *Journal of Adolescent & Adult Literacy, 46*(8), 684–693.

Smith, D., Fisher, D., & Frey, N. (2015). *Better than carrots or sticks: Restorative practices for positive classroom management.* Alexandria, VA: ASCD.

Steele, J. S., Pepper, M. J., Springer, M. G., & Lockwood, J. R. (2015). The distribution and mobility of effective teachers: Evidence from a large, urban school district. *Economics of Education Review, 4,* 86–101.

Stevens, J. E. (2012, May 31). Massachusetts, Washington state lead U.S. trauma movement. *ACES Too High News.* Retrieved from https://acestoohigh.com/2012/05/31/massachusetts-washington-state-lead-u-s-trauma-sensitive-school-movement/

Tomlinson, C. A. (2014). *The differentiated classroom: Responding to the needs of all learners* (2nd ed.). Alexandria, VA: ASCD.

Truebridge, S. R., & Benard, B. (2013, September). Reflections on resilience. *Educational Leadership, 71*(1), 66–67.

Tschannen-Moran, M., & Hoy, W. K. (2000). A multidisciplinary analysis of the nature, meaning, and measurement of trust. *Review of Educational Research, 70*(4), 547–593.

U.S. Department of Education. (2016). *Chronic absenteeism in the nation's schools: 2013–14 civil rights data collection.* Retrieved from http://www2.ed.gov/datastory/chronicabsenteeism.html?src=pr

U.S. Department of Education Office for Civil Rights. (2014, March). *Data snapshot: School discipline, issue brief 1.* Retrieved from http://ocrdata.ed.gov/Downloads/CRDC-School-Discipline-Snapshot.pdf

U.S. Department of Education Office for Civil Rights. (2016). *2013–2014 civil rights data collection: A first look: Key data highlights on equity and opportunity gaps in our nation's public schools.* Retrieved from http://www2.ed.gov/about/offices/list/ocr/docs/2013-14-first-look.pdf

van der Kolk, B. (2014). *The body keeps the score: Brain, mind, and body in the healing of trauma.* New York: Viking.

Vandecandelaere, M., Vansteelandt, S., De Fraine, B., & Van Damme, J. (2016). The effects of early grade retention: Effect modification by prior achievement and age. *Journal of School Psychology, 54*, 77–93.

Weis, L., Eisenhart, M., Cipollone, K., Stich, A. E., Nikischer, A. B., Hanson, J., Ohle Leibrandt, S., Allen, C. D., & Dominguez, R. (2015). In the guise of STEM education reform: Opportunity structures and outcomes in inclusive STEM-focused high schools. *American Educational Research Journal, 52*(6), 1024–1059.

Willems, M. (2003). *Don't let the pigeon drive the bus!* New York: Hyperion.

Wlodkowski, R. J. (1983). *The MOST program: Motivational opportunities for successful teaching.* Phoenix, AZ: Universal Dimensions.

Zander, R. S., & Zander, B. (2000). *The art of possibility: Transforming professional and personal life.* Cambridge, MA: Harvard Business School Press.

Index

About the Authors

Dominique Smith is the director of student services at Health Sciences High & Middle College, where he also serves as a culture builder and student advocate. He is the co-author of *Better Than Carrots or Sticks: Restorative Practices for Positive Classroom Management* and holds a master's degree in social work from the University of Southern California. He received the National School Safety Award from the School Safety Advocacy Council. He can be reached at dsmith@hshsmc.org.

Nancy Frey is a professor of educational leadership at San Diego State University (SDSU) and a teacher leader at Health Sciences High & Middle College. Before joining the university faculty, Frey was a special education teacher in the Broward County (Florida) Public Schools, where she taught students at the elementary and middle school levels. She later worked for the Florida Department of Education on a statewide project for supporting students with disabilities in a general education curriculum. Frey is a recipient of the Christa McAuliffe Award for Excellence in Teacher Education from the American Association of State Colleges and Universities and the Early Career Award from the Literacy Research Association. Her research interests include reading and literacy, assessment, intervention, and curriculum design. She has published many articles and books on literacy and instruction, including *Better Learning Through Structured Teaching* and *How to Reach the Hard to Teach*. She can be reached at nfrey@mail.sdsu.edu.

 **Ian Pumpian** is a professor of educational leadership at San Diego State University and has taught, supervised, and chaired dissertations of several San Diego lead principals and area superintendents. He cofounded Health Sciences High & Middle College and currently serves as the CEO/president. Pumpian served as the executive director of the City Heights Educational Collaborative, where he assumed superintendent-level responsibilities for the educational programs of more than 5,300 students, professional development for their 300+ teachers, and a comprehensive professional development school that annually involved more than 125,000 hours of SDSU faculty and student credential and advanced degree teaching, research, and practical activities. Pumpian has authored and co-authored numerous journal articles and books including *How to Create a Culture of Achievement in Your Classroom or School*. He can be reached at ipumpian@mail.sdsu.edu.

 **Douglas Fisher** is a professor of educational leadership at San Diego State University and a teacher leader at Health Sciences High & Middle College. He is a member of the California Reading Hall of Fame and is the recipient of a Celebrate Literacy Award from the International Reading Association, the Farmer Award for Excellence in Writing from the National Council of Teachers of English, and a Christa McAuliffe Award for Excellence in Teacher Education from the American Association of State Colleges and Universities. He has published numerous articles on improving student achievement, and his books include *The Purposeful Classroom, Enhancing RTI,* and *Intentional and Targeted Teaching*. He can be reached at dfisher@mail.sdsu.edu.

Related ASCD Resources: Equity

At the time of publication, the following ASCD resources were available (ASCD stock numbers appear in parentheses). For up-to-date information about ASCD resources, go to www.ascd.org. You can search the complete archives of *Educational Leadership* at www.ascd.org/el.

ASCD Edge Group

Exchange ideas and connect with other educators interested on the social networking site ASCD EDge® at http://ascdedge.ascd.org.

ASCD myTeachSource®

Download resources from a professional learning platform with hundreds of research-based best practices and tools for your classroom at http://myteachsource.ascd.org.

Online Courses

Embracing Diversity: Effective Teaching (2nd ed.) (#PD11OC123M)
Inclusion: The Basics (2nd ed.) (#PD11OC121)
Teaching with Poverty in Mind (#PD11OC139M)

Print Products

Better Than Carrots or Sticks: Restorative Practices for Positive Classroom Management by Dominique Smith, Douglas Fisher, and Nancy Frey (#116005)

Enhancing RTI: How to Ensure Success with Effective Classroom Instruction and Intervention by Douglas Fisher and Nancy Frey (#110037)

Excellence Through Equity: Five Principles of Courageous Leadership to Guide Achievement for Every Student by Allan M. Blankstein and Pedro Noguera with Lorena Kelly (#116070)

Detracking for Excellence and Equity by Carol Corbett Burris and Delia T. Garrity (#108013)

Inclusion Dos, Don'ts, and Do Betters (Quick Reference Guide) by Toby Karten (#QRG116082)

Leading an Inclusive School: Access and Success for All Students by Richard A. Villa and Jacqueline S. Thousand (#116022)

Learning in the Fast Lane: 8 Ways to Put All Students on the Road to Academic Success by Suzy Pepper Rollins (#114026)

Teaching English Language Learners Across the Content Areas by Judie Haynes and Debbie Zacarian (#109032)

Teaching with Poverty in Mind: What Being Poor Does to Kids' Brains and What Schools Can Do About It by Eric Jenson (#109074)

Turning High-Poverty Schools into High-Performing Schools by William H. Parrett and Kathleen M. Budge (#109003)

For more information: send e-mail to member@ascd.org; call 1-800-933-2723 or 703-578-9600, press 2; send a fax to 703-575-5400; or write to Information Services, ASCD, 1703 N. Beauregard St., Alexandria, VA 22311-1714 USA.